1,000,000 Books

are available to read at

---◆---

www.ForgottenBooks.com

---◆---

Read online
Download PDF
Purchase in print

ISBN 978-1-330-80785-9
PIBN 10108040

This book is a reproduction of an important historical work. Forgotten Books uses
state-of-the-art technology to digitally reconstruct the work, preserving the original format
whilst repairing imperfections present in the aged copy. In rare cases, an imperfection in
the original, such as a blemish or missing page, may be replicated in our edition. We do,
however, repair the vast majority of imperfections successfully; any imperfections that
remain are intentionally left to preserve the state of such historical works.

1 MONTH OF
FREE
READING

at
www.ForgottenBooks.com

By purchasing this book you are
eligible for one month membership to
ForgottenBooks.com, giving you
unlimited access to our entire
collection of over 1,000,000 titles via
our web site and mobile apps.

To claim your free month visit:

www.forgottenbooks.com/free108040

English
Français
Deutsche
Italiano
Español
Português

www.forgottenbooks.com

Mythology Photography **Fiction**
Fishing Christianity **Art** Cooking
Essays Buddhism Freemasonry
Medicine **Biology** Music **Ancient**
Egypt Evolution Carpentry Physics
Dance Geology **Mathematics** Fitness
Shakespeare **Folklore** Yoga Marketing
Confidence Immortality Biographies
Poetry **Psychology** Witchcraft
Electronics Chemistry History **Law**
Accounting **Philosophy** Anthropology
Alchemy Drama Quantum Mechanics
Atheism Sexual Health **Ancient History**
Entrepreneurship Languages Sport
Paleontology Needlework Islam
Metaphysics Investment Archaeology
Parenting Statistics Criminology
Motivational

THE

REBELLION IN THE UNITED STATES;

OR,

THE WAR OF 1861;

BEING A

Complete History of its Rise and Progress,

COMMENCING WITH

THE PRESIDENTIAL ELECTION.

CONTAINING AN ACCOUNT

MOVEMENT OF TROOPS; DESCRIPTION OF BATTLES; LIST OF KILLED AND
WOUNDED; BURNING OF BRIDGES; BURIAL OF SOLDIERS; PATRIOTIC
SPEECHES; AND OTHER INCIDENTS OF INTEREST CON-

THE

REBELLION IN THE UNITED STATES;

OR,

THE WAR OF 1861;

BEING A

Complete History of its Rise and Progress,

COMMENCING WITH

THE PRESIDENTIAL ELECTION.

CONTAINING AN ACCOUNT OF THE

MOVEMENT OF TROOPS; DESCRIPTION OF BATTLES; LIST OF KILLED AND
WOUNDED; BURNING OF BRIDGES; BURIAL OF SOLDIERS; PATRIOTIC
SPEECHES; AND OTHER INCIDENTS OF INTEREST CON-
NECTED WITH THE REBELLION.

TAKEN FROM

GOVERNMENT DOCUMENTS AND OTHER RELIABLE SOURCES.

INTRODUCTION.

In offering to the public this work on the " Rebellion in the United States, " it is done with not a little embarrassment, and many fears and anxieties, known only to those who, for the first time in their life, under their own real signature, have brought before the public, to any considerable extent, the effusions of their pen.

In bringing this little volume before the people, the authoress lays no claim to rare talents, or great abilities as a " historian," nor expects to win unheard-of laurels; but to give to the world a plain, simple, unvarnished account of passing events as they actually occur ; and she has endeavored in this work to " separate the wheat from the chaff," or, in other words, to give the truth in its purity, and cast aside the fiction.

In submitting this work to the criticism of the press and the people, it is done with a thorough knowledge of her own incompetency,. and she is fully aware that abler pens than hers are being wielded in the work of narrating this stupendous rebellion.*

In preparing this " History," the authoress has endeavored, for the time being, as far as possible, to divest

herself of prejudice, or at least to disguise her own
real sentiments, and stand upon " neutral ground," which
is the only true position of the " historian," and to give
only facts, without regard to party or political bearing,—
writing not to win the friendship of any, but hoping for
the favor of all. To record the circumstances, and give
an account of the revolution as it is, the vastness of its
field of operations renders it a work of great labor to
produce a history which shall be at once clear and
minute, and such a one as shall be worthy to be
preserved for generations yet to come, as well as a repos-
itory of the events of the time.

Professing to stand in the shade of obscurity, and
sending forth this volume to tell its own story of the
" Rebellion," the writer leaves it to the sound judgment
of an enlightened public to approve or condemn.

In conclusion, the authoress submits this her first
edition on the " Rebellion " to that " august tribunal,"
the reading public of the nineteenth century, and can
but express the hope that the eye of the critic will glance
lightly over it, and the learned and able of the press
will touch it with a gentle hand, for on them, in a
great measure, depends the success of this work ; therefore hoping they will give it a careful perusal, and speak
of it according to its just merits.

J. B. F.

CONTENTS.

CHAPTER I.

CHAPTER II.

CHAPTER III.

CHAPTER IV.

CHAPTER V.

CHAPTER VI.

CHAPTER VII.

CHAPTER VIII.

CHAPTER IX.

CHAPTER X.

THE

REBELLION IN THE UNITED STATES.

CHAPTER I.

Has our love all died out; have its altars grown cold;
Has the curse come at last which our fathers foretold?
BROTHER JONATHAN'S LAMENT.

THE smouldering fires which for the last thirty years have been secretly burning in the hearts of Southern politicians have, at last, found vent, and, notwithstanding all the peace policies and measures of "conciliation" extended to them by the North, they have chosen to "rebel" against the government of the United States, and to trample upon that noblest charter of liberty which the world has ever seen, framed by our forefathers, and sealed with their blood,—the Constitution of the United States; and the last presidential campaign served to give them a single thread on which to suspend their disunion sentiments, and afford them a plea, though a miserable one, for declaring themselves no longer subject to the federal government, but free to found for themselves a "confederacy" where their own ambitious sons could obtain high official positions, for which they eagerly and impatiently thirsted, and which, under the federal government, for the next four years at least, was denied them. After the reins of government had been, with one or two exceptions, in the hands of the South for many succeeding years, it was deemed by the North that a change would be productive of much good, and result in

11

untold benefits to the whole nation; consequently, into the masses of the North was instilled the "Republican sentiment;" and the nomination of Abraham Lincoln for President of the United States was received with general dissatisfaction throughout the entire South, claiming that his "principles" were adverse to their interests. The "rabid" politicians of the North were touching every chord that would vibrate through the hearts of the people and secure a Republican administration; while the hot-blooded demagogues of the South were stirring up the people and inciting them to "rebellion" and treachery against the general government in the event of the defeat of their candidate for the presidency.

November 6th, being the presidential election day, the following candidates were before the people, viz.: Abraham Lincoln, Republican, of Illinois, for President; Hannibal Hamlin, of Maine, for Vice-President; Stephen A. Douglas, Democrat, of Illinois, for President, and Herschel V. Johnson, of Georgia, Vice-President; John J. Breckenridge, Democrat, of Kentucky, for President, and Joseph Lane, of Oregon, Vice-President; John Bell, unionist, of Tennessee, for President, and Edward Everett, of Massachusetts, Vice-President. The election resulted in Mr. Lincoln's triumph. Seventeen States out of thirty-three cast their majority vote for Lincoln electors, eleven were for Breckenridge, three for Bell, while Douglas received the vote of Missouri and three-sevenths of the vote of New Jersey.

When the news was made known of the election of Mr. Lincoln to the presidential chair, that the Republican star was in the ascendant, it was received at the South with loud demonstrations, and threats of disunion, civil war, and bloodshed, which savored more of "conspiracies" than of statemanship or honest aims, and which was secretly responded to by many traitorous spirits at the North.

First and foremost in the rebellion, South Carolina took the lead, and, on the 20th of December, 1860, declared herself out of the Union, and a free and independent State, and was immediately followed by Mississippi, Florida, Alabama, Georgia, Louisiana, North Carolina, and Texas, forming themselves into a confederacy with their capital at Montgomery, Alabama, and Jefferson Davis as their president, who, with Governor Pickens and some other turbulent spirits among the revolutionists, seemed almost entirely lost to considerations of prudence and discretion, and to act upon the supposition that the loyal States could be bullied into a conflict or frightened into "submission" with their threatened thunder and smoke of war.

But the North remained cool and firm, thinking that when error and passion had ceased to declaim, perhaps truth might be heard, and an amicable adjustment of difficulties might be arrived at; compromise after compromise was drawn up, and Congress was active in its efforts to repair the breach between the States, and restore peace and union where now was alienation and discord; but all to no purpose; in that hotbed of secession and treachery the voice of conciliation, in any form whatever, could not even gain a hearing, and the new confederacy, so belligerent in spirit, and apparently eager for the fight, would accept of no compromise, while the free States, conscious of their strength and resources, were peaceful in their inclinations, and reluctant to resort to coercion.

The news of the election of Lincoln was received at the North by many with demonstrations of rejoicing, but their joy was soon turned to sadness, for it was immediately followed by a general suspension of business; no trade; credit almost destroyed; awful panic in the money market, that commodity bringing exorbitant rates of interest, and could only be procured by such as could give about three times its value in collaterals; great declension in the

2

manufacturing districts; nearly all mills and manufactories were either entirely closed or were working on short time, and thousands were thus deprived of work or any means of subsistence for themselves and families, with the wants and necessities of a "Northern winter" staring them full in the face, and but little hopes of a speedy termination of difficulties.

November 22d all the banks in the District of Columbia, and also those in Philadelphia, Baltimore, Wheeling, and Norfolk, Va., together with the Farmers' and Exchange Bank in Charleston, S. C., suspended specie payments.

23d, the banks of Augusta, Ga., Trenton, N. J., and Pittsburg, Penn., suspended specie payments.

26th, all the principal banks of Tennessee, including the State Bank, suspended specie payments.

The twenty-ninth of November was observed, in most of the Northern States, as a day of thanksgiving and prayer; sermons were preached by many eminent divines, generally urging a policy of peace, concession, and fraternization in the great questions of the day.

The eyes of the masses of the North were now turned, with an imploring look, towards Congress, with the hope that that body, when convened, would take some measures to avert the impending blow which seemed ready to fall upon us, and calm the troubled waters of political discord, and restore peace and unity.

On the twenty-seventh of November a special session of the Legislature of Maryland was called for, which Governor Hicks refused to convene, and wrote a letter in reply, taking strong grounds against secession, and declared his purpose was to avoid any precipitation of his State in action on the part of secessionists.

December 3d, Congress met at Washington; the House opened at twelve o'clock, with the following impressive and eloquent prayer for the Union, by the Chaplain of the House, the Rev. Mr. Stockton: —

"O God! we remember the past, and we are grateful for the past. We thank thee for the discovery of this New World; we thank thee for the colonization of our part of it; we thank thee for the establishment of our National Independence; we thank thee for the organization of our National Union; we thank thee for all the blessings we have enjoyed within this Union, — national blessings, civil blessings, social blessings, spiritual blessings, all kinds of blessings, unspeakably great and precious blessings, such blessings as were never enjoyed by any other people since the world began. And now, O Lord, our God, we offer to thee our humble praise for the past, the present; and for all the future will it please thee, for Christ's sake, to grant us thy special aid. Thou art very high and lifted up; thou lookest down over the whole land, from lake to gulf, from sea to sea, from the rising of the sun to the going down thereof; and thou knowest all our doings, and thou knowest all our failings; thou knowest that our good men are at fault, and that our wise men are at fault, in the North and in the South, in the East and in the West,— they are all at fault; we know not what is best for us to do, and with common consent we come to thee, O Lord, our God; and we pray thee to overrule all unreasonable and wicked men, in all parts of our confederacy. We pray thee to inspire, and to strengthen, and to assist all true patriots in every part of the Union; may thy blessing rest upon all departments of our government. We remember, with especial solicitude, the President of these United States, and his immediate advisers. They lack wisdom, but if they call upon thee thou wilt give them wisdom, for thou givest it to all men liberally, and upbraideth not. Whilst we trust that they pray for themselves, we here, also, pray for them; let thy Holy Spirit be granted unto them, and grant that they may speedily see what is exactly right for them to do, and grant them grace to do it, and to fully understand the position in which they are placed. We thank thee for this bright and beautiful morning; for the assembling of the two Houses of Congress; we pray that thy blessing may rest on the Vice-President, and upon every senator in his place; upon the Speaker of the House, and upon every member in his place. We rejoice to learn that they see their responsibilities, and that they feel their responsibilities, and that many of them are looking towards thee for counsel and direction. O Lord, our God, let thy own presence subdue every heart, every mind; and sanctify all actions to thy own glory and the greatness of our whole people; and O grant that we may still live in peace and harmony in this blessed Union. Amen."

The roll of members was then called. Most of the States were fully represented; to the surprise of some, every member from South Carolina, except one (Mr. Bonham), answered to his name on roll-call in the House. But no senators were present from South Carolina, Georgia, or Louisiana, — the South Carolina senators, Chesnut and Hammond, having resigned their seats in the Senate, the former on the tenth, and the latter on the eleventh, of the previous month (November).

We are compelled, though painfully and reluctantly, to yield to the force of concurring evidence, establishing the fact that treachery and treason has struck at the very root of the Federal Government.

The solicitude and impatience of the people, generally, to see or hear the presidential message, was intense; hoping, and clinging to that hope with the tenacity of life, that it might contain measures of compromise which would forever settle the question of disunion, and leave the country unscathed by the terrible ravages of civil war.

The message could not be transmitted to Congress at the opening of the session, simply because fair manuscript copies for each House could not be made out in time, without employing the clerks on Sunday.

Early on the morning of the third the President dispatched Mr. Trescott, Assistant Secretary of State, to Charleston, with the message, and to urge a postponement of action, in regard to secession, until Congress could act on compromises and remedies; who, after an absence of seven days, returns and immediately resigns his office. At twelve o'clock, on the 4th, the President's message was delivered to both Houses of Congress, and the department reports sent in. The message takes strong grounds for conciliation; blames the North for its aggressions on slavery; proposes plans of compromise; recommends amendments to the Constitution; denies the right of secession, yet disparages coercion. Its reading was listened to with the most profound attention, yet it did not satisfy the South, nor please the North; it was attacked fiercely in the Senate by Clingman, of North Carolina, and defended by Crittenden, of Kentucky. Southern senators declare the message to be weak, vacillating, inconsistent and untrue; while the leading Republican senators were united and unhesitating in pronouncing it a weak, silly paper, unworthy such a man at such a time. Evidently it was not what was expected; at the time of our country's greatest peril something more decisive was hoped for.

It was charged by some that the President secretly favored secession, and *quietly* responded to the calls of the South, made upon the government, and if not actually assisting in the movement, at least doing nothing to hinder it. " He that is not for me is against me."

Then it was urged by the friends of Mr. Buchanan that, as his term of office had nearly expired, he declined to act, choosing rather to leave the settlement of all national difficulties to the incoming administration — peaceful imbecility! How long, think you, my readers, would the " hero of New Orleans," the immortal Jackson, have sat with his arms folded and his eyes closed, patiently waiting

2*

for the time to arrive when he should retire, and leave his successor to settle difficulties as best he could? "In the field of argument, or on the field of battle," would he not spring to his feet (as on a former occasion), and with the words—"By the Eternal, I take the responsibility!" —employ all his powers to suppress the rebellion, though the people of his own native State were the prime movers in it?

In the House, Mr. Boteler, of Virginia, offered a resolution to appoint a special committee, of one from each State, to whom should be referred so much of the President's message as "relates to the present perilous condition of the country." The United States Senate, December 4th, was characterized by the most exciting speeches of Southern senators, looking to secession as their only relief from Northern domination. In the House, on the question of referring the secession matter in the message to a special committee, the declaration of Mr. Miles, of South Carolina, that his State was already out of the confederacy, in everything but form; of Mr. Hawkins, of Florida, that the day of compromises was passed forever; of Mr. Singleton, of Mississippi, that his State could take care of herself; of Mr. Pugh, of Alabama, that the Union was virtually dissolved; of Mr. Jones, of Georgia, that his State was prepared to go out of the confederacy; and of other southerners to a similar effect, produced but little sensation. There was a slight startle upon the announcement of Mr. Miles, " that his State was out of the Union," and the inquiry was made, in the gallery, why he and his colleagues were occupying seats in the national capitol. The answer to this question was—To get their money and stationery.

December 5th, at the meeting of the State Electoral Colleges, Abraham Lincoln, for President, and Hannibal Hamlin, for Vice-President, received the votes of seventeen States, or one hundred and eighty electoral votes.

On the sixth, the Speaker of the United States House of Representatives announced the committee of thirty-three, called for under Mr. Boteler's resolution, to consider " so much of the President's message as relates to the present perilous condition of the country." The names are as follows: — Ohio, Mr. Corwin, chairman; Virginia, Mr. Millson ; Massachusetts, Mr. Adams ; North Carolina, Mr. Winslow; New York, Mr. Humphreys; South Carolina, Mr. Boyce ; Pennsylvania, Mr. Campbell ; Georgia, Mr. Love; Connecticut, Mr. Ferry ; Maryland, Mr. Davis ; Rhode Island, Mr. Robinson ; •Delaware, Mr. Whiteley ; New Hampshire, Mr. Tappan ; New Jersey, Mr. Stratton ; Kentucky, Mr. Bristow ; Vermont, Mr. Morrill ; Tennessee, Mr. Nelson ; Indiana, Mr. Dunn ; Louisiana, Mr. Taylor ; Mississippi, Mr. Davis ; Illinois, Mr. Kellogg ; Alabama, Mr. Houston ; Maine, Mr. Morse ; Missouri, Mr. Phelps ; Arkansas, Mr. Rust ; Michigan, Mr. Howard ; Florida, Mr. Hawkins ; Texas, Mr. Hamilton ; Wisconsin, Mr. Washburne ; Iowa, Mr. Curtis ; California, Mr. Burch ; Minnesota, Mr. Windom ; Oregon, Mr. Stout.

When the reading of the names was concluded, Mr. Hawkins, the only representative from 'Florida, asked to be excused from serving on the committee, and, declining to act, was approached in a solemn and patriotic speech, by John Cochrane, of New York; who, figuratively, with the American flag in one hand and a splendid spread eagle in the other, appealed to the Florida member to act upon the committee. It was a burst of thrilling eloquence, and the applause in the galleries attested the sincerity with which the popular heart cherishes the love of the Union; but Hawkins heeded not the appeal, and before the House had an opportunity to act upon the subject, on motion of Mr. Millson, of Virginia, that body adjourned, leaving Mr. Hawkins in suspense, and securing to Mr. Millson a volley of curses for his interference. Subsequently Mr. Hawkins excused himself for not serv-

ing on the committee of thirty-three, in an elaborate
speech, defending the South and the right of secession,
and declaring the appointment of the committee to be a
constructive fraud, as some persons believed it to be a
great pacificator, to heal our wounds and produce a political millennium.   The effect, if carried out, would be to
demoralize and degrade the South.   He was sorry the
proposition came from one of the noble sons of the South ;
denouncing the Union and Union-saving committee in no
measured terms ; rejecting the very idea of compromise,
and added that he was not acting under impulse, but
from convictions of twenty years.

In addition to Mr. Hawkins, Mr. Boyce, of South Carolina, and Mr. Morrill, of Vermont, asked to be excused,
but were promptly refused by the House.   Mr. Hawkins
rose and signified that he wished to say, with all defer-
ence, " that he would not serve ; " accordingly the " sons
of the South " withdrew.

Very little importance was attached to the committee
of thirty-three, appointed to save the Union, as the very
basis upon which it was constructed would defeat the object in view ; it being composed of discordant elements,
there could be no concerted action.

On the tenth of December a special cabinet meeting
was called by the President, at which Howell Cobb, Secretary of the Treasury, resigned ; after several ineffectual
attempts to extricate the treasury from its tangled condition, and failing to account for the disbursement of
large sums of government money, he proposed to resign
at once ; and his resignation was accepted.

We find, bearing the same date, a long and hot-headed
letter, written by Secretary Cobb to the people of Georgia,
in which, after referring to the origin and purposes of the
Republican party, he says : — " It is not simply that a
comparatively obscure abolitionist, who hates the institution of the South, has been elected President, and that

we are asked to live under the administration of a man who commands neither our respect nor confidence, that the South-contemplates resistance, even to disunion; wounded honor might tolerate the outrage, until, by another vote of the people, the nuisance could be abated; but the election of Mr. Lincoln involves far higher considerations. It brings to the South the solemn judgment of a majority of the people of every Northern State, with a solitary exception, in favor of doctrines and principles violative of her constitutional rights, humiliating to her pride, destructive of her equality in the Union, and fraught with the greatest danger to the peace and safety of her people. The question is now presented, whether a longer submission to an increasing spirit and power of aggression is compatible either with her honor or her safety. In my mind there is no room for doubt. The issue must now be met, or forever abandoned; equality and safety in the Union are at an end, and it only remains to be seen whether our manhood is equal to the task of asserting and maintaining independence out of it. The Union formed by our fathers was one of equality, justice and fraternity; on the fourth of March it will be supplanted by a Union of sectionalism and hatred. Black Republicanism is the ruling sentiment at the North. They have trampled upon the Constitution of Washington and Madison, and will prove equally faithless to their pledges; you ought not, cannot trust them. We are no longer brethren, dwelling together in unity; they have buried brotherhood in the same grave with the Constitution;" — and concludes by saying, —

"Fellow-citizens of Georgia: I have endeavored to place before you the facts of the case in plain and unimpassioned language; and I should feel that I had done injustice to my own convictions, and been unfaithful to you, if I did not, in conclusion, warn you against the danger of delay, and impress upon you the hopelessness of any remedy for these evils, short of secession. You have to deal with a shrewd, heartless and unscrupulous enemy, who, in their extremity, may promise anything, but in the end will do nothing. On the 4th day of March, 1861, the federal government will pass into the hands of the abolitionists; it will then cease to have the claim either upon your confidence or your loyalty; and in my honest judgment, each hour that Georgia remains, thereafter, a member of the Union, will be an hour of degradation, to be followed by certain, speedy ruin. I entertain no doubt either of your right or duty to secede from the Union. Arouse, then, all your manhood for the great work before you, and be prepared, on that day, to announce and maintain your independence out of the Union; for you will never again have equality and justice in it. Identified with you in heart, feeling and interest, I return to share in whatever destiny the future has in store for our State and ourselves."

Self-sacrificing man! his "*interest*," possibly, may be in Georgia; an empty treasury offers *him* no inducements to remain at the national capital, and feeling so keenly the "danger of delay," and the "*degradation*" of remaining in the Union, he should have tendered his resignation at an earlier day.

Mr. Toucey, Secretary of the Navy, was called upon to act in his stead, *ad interim*, and three days after, Mr. Phillip F. Thomas, ex-Governor of Maryland, was nominated and confirmed Secretary of the Treasury, vice Cobb, resigned.

On the 13th, the sentiments of the people of Philadelphia were expressed by an immense Union demonstration, by proclamation of the mayor.

On the same day the cabinet, at Washington, was the scene of contention and strife; exciting speeches were made in regard to the re-enforcement of Fort Moultrie, in Charleston harbor, in command of Major Robert Anderson, (whither he had been sent, on the 18th of November, to relieve Col. Gardiner, who was ordered to Texas). The President opposed its re-enforcement, expressing his " determination " to send no more troops to the forts near Charleston, saying he had " assurances " that the fort would not be attacked, if no re-enforcements were attempted, and that everything should be done, on his part, to avoid a collision. Mr. Cass, Secretary of State, and Mr. Toucey, Secretary of the Navy, both strenuously urged the policy of strengthening Major Anderson fully. Gen. Cass said,—" These forts must be strengthened ; I demand it." The President replied, — " I am sorry to differ from the Secretary of the State, but the interests of the country do not demand a re-enforcement of the forts at Charleston ; I cannot do it ; I take the responsibility." The next day Secretary Cass resigned.

The commander who deliberately leaves an insufficient garrison in a fort, without re-enforcing, or attempting to re-enforce, that garrison, by such acts of omission and commission palpably " *challenges* " the enemy ; and yet our trembling President, afraid of his own shadow, where the vaporing South is concerned, but reckless of decency where the North is interested, is *afraid* to strengthen his own forts for *fear* the South should *take offence !* What a military commander Mr. Buchanan would make. How must the bones of George Washington, Andrew Jackson, and Zachary Taylor writhe in their graves ! not dare to strengthen our own forts, for fear the enemy should be offended ! How shall we be regarded, or respected, by the military nations of Europe hereafter ? Such *cowardice* is a blot upon every American citizen. A clergyman, visiting a school connected with the alms-house, in a small village in Massachusetts, made some remarks to the children, in which he endeavored to illustrate the sinful condition of men, in a familiar way. " You know," said the clergyman, " that the negroes at the South are serving their masters.   Now, we, sinful creatures, are serving a master who is worse than a slave-driver; and can any boy tell me who this master is?"   "Yes, sir," said one of the lads, with a great deal of emphasis, " it is James Buchanan."

The following letter, from the wife of an officer at Fort Moultrie, tells its own story : —

"FORT MOULTRIE, December 11, 1860.

"DEAR—— : I feel too indignant; I can hardly stand the way in which this little garrison is treated by the heads of government.   Troops and proper accommodation are positively refused; and yet, the commander has orders to hold and defend the fort.   Was ever such sacrifice (an intentional one) known?   The Secretary has sent several officers, at different times, to inspect here, as if that helped; it is a mere sham, to make believe he will do something.   In the mean time a crisis is very near; I am to go to Charleston the first of the week.   Within a few days, we hear — and from so many sources that we cannot doubt it — that the Charlestonians are erecting two batteries, one just opposite us, at a little village, Mount Pleasant, and another on the end of this island; and they dare the commander to interfere, while they are getting ready to *fight sixty men!*   In this weak little fort, I suppose, President Buchanan and Secretary Floyd intend the Southern Confederacy to be cemented with the blood of this brave little garrison.   These names should be handed down to the end of time.

" When the last man is shot down, I presume they will think of sending troops.   The soldiers here deserve great credit; though they know what an unequal number is coming to massacre them, yet they are in good spirits, and will fight desperately.   Our commander says he never saw such a brave little band.   I feel desperate myself. Our only hope is in God.   My love to all.

"Your affectionate sister."

CHAPTER II.

Inaction now is crime. The old earth reels,
Inebriate with guilt; and Vice, grown bold,
Laughs Innocence to scorn. The thirst for gold
Hath made men demons.   BURLEIGH.

THE entire force of the United States troops, stationed in the Southern States, at this time, was as follows: —

At Fort Monroe, Virginia, eight companies of artillery; at Fayetteville Arsenal, North Carolina, one company of artillery; Key West, Florida, one company of artillery; at Fort Moultrie, South Carolina, two companies of artillery; at Augusta, Georgia, one company of artillery; Barrancas Barracks, near Pensacola, Florida, one company of artillery; Baton Rouge, Louisiana, one company of artillery; total, about eight hundred men; and about one hundred and twenty United States marines at Norfolk and Pensacola.

December 14th, Lewis Cass, Secretary of State, resigned his seat in the cabinet. The reasons and motives which prompted his resignation are probably not perfectly understood; though it is supposed it was owing to his disapproval of the President's inaction in regard to re-enforcing Southern forts, arsenals, navy yards, etc. His resignation caused much feeling and comment. Especially was the President grave, almost to sadness. The withdrawal of his long-tried and cherished friend from his bosom councils added poignancy to his sorrow, which was difficult to overcome. President Buchanan issued a proclamation, calling upon the people of the Union, in view of the distracted and dangerous condition of the

3   25

country, to observe the 4th of January, 1861, as a day of
fasting, humiliation and prayer.

> A gale came up from the sou'-sou'-west,
>   'Twas fierce November weather;
> But the ship had felt such a storm before,
>   And her planks still held together.
> And thus, though the howling tempest showed
>   No signs of diminution,
> The passengers said, " We'll trust our ship,
>   The staunch old Constitution! "
>
> The captain stood on the quarter-deck —
>   " The seas," he said, " they batter us;
> 'Twas my watch below in the former gale —
>   I doubt if we'll weather Hatteras.
> The wind on the one side blows me off,
>   The current sets me shoreward;
> I'll just lay-to between them both
>   And *seem* to be going forward."
>
> " Breakers ahead! " cried the watch on the bow;
>   " Hard up! " was the first mate's order;
> " She feels the ground-swell," the passengers cried,
>   " And the seas already board her! "
> The foresail split in the angry gust;
>   In the hold the ballast shifted;
> And an old tar said, " If Jackson steered
>   We shouldn't thus have drifted! "
>
> But the captain cried, " Let go your helm! "
>   And then he called to the bo'swain,
> " Pipe all hands to the quarter-deck,
>   And we'll save her by devotion! "
> The first mate hurled his trumpet down;
>   The old tars cursed together,
> To see the good ship helpless roll
>   At the sport of wave and weather.
>
> The tattered sails are all aback,
>   Yards crack, and masts are started;
> And the captain weeps and says his prayers,
>   Till the hull be mid-ships parted;
> But God is on the steersman's side —
>   The crew are in revolution;
> The wave that washes the captain off
>   Will save the Constitution!
>   BAYARD TAYLOR.

On the 15th, Attorney-General Black was appointed Secretary of State, in place of Lewis Cass, resigned.

On the 18th of December, Senator Crittenden, of Kentucky, introduced into the United States Senate resolutions of compromise, as a settlement of differences between the Slave and Free States. The bill, as introduced, proposed to renew the Missouri compromise line, prohibiting slavery in the territory north of 36 degrees 30 minutes, and protecting it south of that latitude; and for the admission of new States, with or without slavery, as their constitutions should provide; to prohibit the abolition of slavery, by Congress, in the States; to prohibit its abolition in the District of Columbia, so long as it exists either in Virginia or Maryland; to permit the transportation of slaves, in any of the States, by land or water; to provide for the payment of fugitive slaves, when rescued; to repeal one obnoxious feature of the fugitive slave law — the inequality of the fee to the commissioner; and, also, to ask the repeal of all the personal liberty bills in the Northern States.

These concessions were submitted, in the form of amendments to the Constitution, to a select Senate committee of thirteen. Much time was consumed in considering various propositions to arrest the progress of dissolution, and give peace to the country. Messrs. Crittenden, Douglas and Bigler maintained it with great zeal and ability. Mr. Douglas declared, if that mode of compromise would not answer he was willing to go for any other, consistent with honor or justice; that he was ready to consider any question for the preservation of the country.

The appeals of Mr. Crittenden, in behalf of the Union, are said to have been eloquent and sublime. He, too, was willing to embrace any other effective mode of adjustment. Mr. Bigler, of Pennsylvania, advocated a final settlement of difficulties, by a division line across the

country, so that the question of slavery could be taken
out of Congress, and entirely separated from the popular
elections at the North, without which we could never have
permanent peace. Messrs. Davis, Toombs and Hunter dis-
cussed the present unhappy condition of the country, and
manifested a willingness to accept any measure of final
settlement which would secure their just rights in the
Union. Though, at the same time, an under-current of
secession feeling was sweeping them steadily on, and blind-
ing them to every concession, or plan of compromise,
which could be made by the North, as they had previously said that the South would have "*no compromise*,"
that the Union was "*virtually dissolved*," that the day
for the adjustment of difficulties was "*passed forever;*"
so, therefore, their action on the committee of thirteen
was mere form, without expecting any beneficial results.
So, accordingly, when the final vote was taken on the
Crittenden proposition, it was defeated.

On the 18th and 19th, Andrew Johnson, United States
Senator from Tennessee, spoke on the resolutions, proposing amendments to the Constitution. He denied the
right of secession, and called upon the President to enforce the laws, regardless of consequences. Taking up
arms to resist the federal laws, he pronounced treason.

December 19th, Governor Hicks, of Maryland, declined
to receive the commissioner from Mississippi. He vindi-
cated the course by expressing strong Union sentiments;
notwithstanding which the commissioner of Mississippi to
Maryland addressed a large meeting in Baltimore, advis-
ing coöperation, on the part of the people of Maryland, in
the secession movement.

December 23d, the excitement, consequent upon the
state of affairs in the nation, was entirely absorbed by an
astounding report of a robbery of Indian Trust Fund
bonds, in the Department of the Interior, committed during Secretary Thompson's visit to North Carolina, as

commissioner on the part of his own State, Mississippi. The amount abstracted is confessed, by Godard Bailey, the guilty disbursing clerk, to have been eight hundred and thirty thousand dollars; but, on investigation, it is believed, " the half has not been told."

Bailey, to whom the bonds were specially intrusted, is a native of South Carolina, but at the time of his appointment, as disbursing clerk, was a citizen of Alabama.

The funds stolen are known as the Indian Trust Fund, which has accumulated, for the benefit of various Indian tribes, under our treaties with them. According to the provision of many of these treaties, a certain sum is stipulated to be paid to the Indians for their land, the sum to be paid in annual payments, equalling, in amount, the interest that would be due upon the principal. In order to avoid the necessity of being compelled to pay these annual sums out of the current receipts of the revenue, the government has been in the habit of investing the principal in State stocks, and making the interest on these stocks meet the annual payment due the Indians.

It was these bonds or stocks, thus acquired, that have been so unlawfully abstracted from the Interior department. The most intense excitement prevailed concerning the robbery. Mr. Floyd, Secretary of War, and several other high officials under government, were charged with " complicity " in the affair, and said to be " *deeply implicated* " in the revelations made. Secretary Thompson appealed to the House for the appointment of a committee, with full power to send for persons and papers, and asked for investigation, by Congress, in order to vindicate his own honor and expose the guilty, that full justice might be done in the premises.

Whether guilty or *not* guilty of the " robbery," is he not equally guilty with Floyd, of maladministration in office ? Was he not a conspirator against the government when he accepted the appointment of commissioner, from

3*

one " *rebellious* " State to another ? Was he attending to
the duties of the office which he still held under government, and by whom he was paid for his services, when
he left Washington, as the bearer of *treasonable* documents from Mississippi to North Carolina, urging the
coöperation of that State in the matter of secession,
and declared that it afforded him "*great pleasure*" to
accept this appointment and obey these instructions?
How came the fraud (which had been going on for many
months) to be discovered just at the time of his absence?
And, yet, this is the man who calls upon Congress to
" *vindicate his honor !* "

Caleb Cushing, special messenger of the President to
South Carolina, to induce the postponement of the adoption of the ordinance of secession, returns and reports the
passage of the ordinance, and reports no hopes of any
arrangement of the pending differences. He represented
the condition of affairs, there, to be fearful and alarming.
A cabinet meeting was then called. A deepening gloom,
darker than the pall of night, and as solemn as the sar-
cophagus of Washington, appears to have settled over the
national capital. The most hopeful were desponding,
seeing no prospect of a settlement of difficulties. There
seemed to be no man, or set of men, equal to the occasion,
though there were some who had the ability, the sagacity,
the statesmanship, to grapple with questions at issue, yet
were powerless to arrest the fearful ruin that impended.
Mr. Crittenden, in conversation with a friend, said that it
was the darkest day of his life ; that he was overwhelmed
with solicitude for his country, and that nothing but the
affection of the people for the Union could restore peace.
Terror and gloom was on every countenance. The Crittenden compromise was defeated by the Senate committee
of thirteen, and the House committee of thirty-three could
accomplish nothing. All confidence in the administration
was lost. A President who was secretly aiding the South,

who violated the Constitution, and refused to administer the laws; who was false to the obligations upon him to preserve our-nationality; — a cabinet composed almost entirely of Southern men, with secession principles, — nothing could be hoped for from that quarter.

The Union, "the old ship of state," which had been steered safely through fogs and darkness, and various dangers, for upwards of three-score years and ten, — which had hitherto weathered every storm, — was now being driven swiftly before wind and tide to the rocks and shoals of civil war; and it was of no avail that the foaming breakers ahead were pointed out to the officers and crew, to whom had been entrusted the management of the noble vessel, with her precious freight of historic glory, present prosperity and power, and all the glowing hopes of future years. Every man seemed drunk or mad, and shipwreck appeared inevitable. Reason and moderation were banished from both sections. The extremists, both North and South, were equally violent; and the United States was precipitated, by reckless politicians, into the most revolutionary condition ever witnessed in any country in the world.

December 24. Intense excitement in Pittsburg, Pennsylvania, in consequence of orders being given to ship, from the Alleghany arsenal, seventy-eight ten and eight-inch columbiads to Fort Newport, near Galveston, and forty-eight to Ship Island, near Balize, at the mouth of the Mississippi, — both unfinished forts. The people regarded the order as designed to strip the arsenal, in order to place the heavy guns in the hands of the enemies of the government. An immense meeting was held in the street, relative to the removal of ordnance South. Several resolutions were adopted, almost unanimously, declaring loyalty to-the Union, deploring the existing state of things, and that it is the special duty of Pennsylvania to look to the fidelity of her sons; and in that view, call on the President, as a citizen of that commonwealth, to see that the public receive no detriment at *his* hands. Yet, notwithstanding the indignation of the people, and their avowed determination to oppose, by force, their removal, on the twenty-eighth the order was carried out. The work of removal commenced; the heavy guns of the arsenal were placed on board of boats, procured for that purpose, and forwarded to their destination, at the South.

On the 24th, the members of Congress from South Carolina notified the Speaker of the House of Representatives, that the secession of their State dissolved their connection with that body. The Speaker directed the names of the South Carolina members to be retained on the roll, and to be regularly called; thus not recognizing the conduct of their State, as severing their connection with the House, or government.

December 26. Ex-Speaker, James L. Orr, R. W. Barnwell, and ex-Governor J. H. Adams, commissioners from South Carolina, appointed to negotiate with the federal government, in relation to matters pertaining to the ordinance of secession adopted by a convention of that State, arrived in Washington, and were received by Mr. Trescott, Assistant Secretary of State (resigned), and who subsequently acts as their secretary.

Col. Myers and Captain Donovan, of South Carolina, and Major Wayne, of Georgia, resigned their offices in the army. On the evening of the same day, December 26, Major Anderson commenced the evacuation of Fort Moultrie, transferring his entire force (about eighty men), with stores, munitions, movable arms, etc., to Fort Sumter, after having spiked the guns and set fire to the gun-carriages. The facts show that Major Robert Anderson, who commanded Fort Moultrie, knowing the position to be untenable, evacuated it and took possession of Fort Sumter, an almost impregnable fort, where, in the event of an attack upon United States property, he would be enabled to defend it against great odds. Anderson withdrew for strategic purposes ; for it was generally known, and the expressed opinion of military men, that Fort Moultrie could not be held, against a resolute attack, for twenty-four hours ; but that Sumter was the strongest fort, of its size, in the world. Thus it will be seen that the evacuation of a weak and comparatively worthless position, for a stronger one, was a wise military movement.

> They stood within those fortress walls,
>   A small but gallant band ;
> O'er them still waved the stars and stripes,
>   Bright emblem of their land.
>
> Scarce there one man to every star
>   This hero band could boast,
> Yet they must guard the banner there
>   Against a countless host.
>
> The chieftain called his men around,
>   And pointing to those stars,
> "Dare you defend them with your lives ?"
>   They answered with huzzas.
>
> His pitying eye o'erlooked his men,
>   Then at the flag on high ;
> A tear stole down his cheek for those
>   That were too brave to die.
>
> "Haul down your colors from the staff,
>   You shall not perish here ;
> It were in vain to ask of you
>   A sacrifice so dear.
>
> On yonder fortress it shall wave,
>   And all the world defy ;
> Then, if your country dares demand,
>   *There* we can nobly die."
>
> The morning sun salutes that flag,
>   Defended by that band ;
> Humanity's great heart sends forth
>   Its plaudits o'er the land.
>
> Our Union banner still shall wave,
>   Each star in bold relief,
> If we but dare defend our flag
>   Like Sumter's gallant chief.

The artificial island on which Fort Sumter is built is constructed of the refuse from the granite quarries of New England. Ten years was consumed in its completion, at a cost of half a million of dollars. The fortification is of a pentagonal form, built of solid brick masonry. The walls are fifty feet in height, and from eight to ten feet in thickness, and are pierced for three tiers of guns, besides having necessary loop-holes for musketry, and designed for an armament of one hundred and forty pieces of ordnance, of all calibres. The full armament of the fort, however, had not arrived there when Major Anderson took possession, but it was thought that, with the armament then in the fort, the guns would be capable of throwing six thousand pounds of shot at each discharge.

The other officers of the garrison, under Major Anderson, were Captain Abner Doubleday, Captain Seymour, Lieutenant T. Talbot, Lieutenant J. C. Davis, Lieutenant N. J. Hall, all of the first regiment, artillery; Captain J. G. Foster, and Lieutenant G. W. Snyder, of the engineer corps; Assistant Surgeon S. W. Crawford, of the medical staff. The force under these gentlemen consisted of two companies of artillery; the companies, however, were not full, the two comprising only about seventy men, including the band.

On the morning of the 27th it was ascertained at Charleston that Fort Moultrie was evacuated. This news was displayed on the bulletins, and intense excitement spread throughout the city; the indignation of the people knew no bounds. Several of the military companies were ordered out, and the convention went into secret session.

The intelligence that Major Anderson had abandoned and destroyed the chief material works of Fort Moultrie was received at Washington before noon on the 27th; but up to ten o'clock, P. M., no official information had been received from Charleston, either by the President or

Secretary of War. At first, the report was discredited, and public opinion was not at all settled upon the point, until, late in the afternoon, the following dispatch was sent to the President, by the South Carolina commissioners, they having just received it : —

" Great excitement, on account of removal of garrison from Fort Moultrie to Fort Sumter. Removed on Wednesday evening, and at night. Captain Foster, with small guard, left in Fort Moultrie to complete dismantling. They are now burning gun-carriages ; guns spiked, and report of intention to blow up Fort Moultrie."

The President immediately convened his cabinet, in extraordinary session. The confirmation of the important intelligence spread with great rapidity, and created most intense excitement throughout the entire country. It was the topic everywhere, and various were the conjectures as to the cause which led to the event. Many approved, and but few condemned. The conduct of Major Anderson was universally commended by Northern men of all parties, and by Union men everywhere.

December 28. The cabinet adjourned, after a protracted and exciting session of six hours. The affair at Charleston was the subject under consideration. Secretary Floyd stated to the President, in writing, that unless Major Anderson was withdrawn from Fort Sumter, he could not remain in the cabinet.

The South Carolina commissioners " *demanded*," as an ultimatum, that the federal troops be withdrawn immediately from all the Charleston forts,— as their presence, pending negotiations, was a menace, — or this would be their last interview, and they would return to South Carolina, and prepare for the worst.

How far they might have succeeded in bullying the President into compliance with their wishes, it is not possible now to say, but for the interference of such men as Holt and Stanton.

Thompson, Floyd and Thomas contended that a quasi-treaty had been made, by the officers of the government, with the leaders of the rebellion, to offer no resistance to their violations of law and seizures of government property. Floyd, especially, blazed with indignation at what he termed the " violation of honor." At last, Mr. Thompson, Secretary of the Interior, formally moved that an imperative order be issued to Major Anderson, to retire from Sumter to Fort Moultrie ; abondoning Sumter to the enemy, and proceeding to a post, where, from the weakness of the position, he must at once surrender. Mr. Stanton, the then newly-appointed Attorney General (now Secretary of War), could sit still no longer; and rising, he said, with all the earnestness that could be expressed in his bold and resolute features,— " Mr. President, it is my duty, as your legal adviser, to say that you have no right to give up the property of the government, or abandon the soldiers of the United States to its enemies ; and the course proposed by the Secretary of the Interior, if followed, is treason, and will involve you, and all concerned, in treason."

Such language had never before been heard in Buchanan's cabinet, and the men who had so long ruled and bullied the President were surprised and enraged to be thus rebuked. Floyd and Thompson sprang to their feet with fierce, menacing gestures, seeming about to assault Stanton. Mr. Holt took a step forward to the side of the Attorney General. The imbecile President implored them, piteously, to take their seats.

The President determined, after a full deliberation, not to withdraw Major Anderson, and Mr. Floyd's resignation was, therefore, accepted. While the cabinet was still in session, news came that Fort Moultrie and Castle Pinckney had been taken possession of by South Carolina militia ; also, Secretary Thomas received a dispatch from Charleston stating that the revenue-cutter Aiken, in the port of Charleston, had been seized by the authorities, and that the captain, M. L. Coste, who is a native of Charleston, had resigned. This intelligence was immediately communicated to the cabinet.

Though the President would not accede to the demands of the commissioners, he signified that Major Anderson, in his movement, acted upon his own responsibility, and without any instructions to that effect; and were he so disposed, subsequent events precluded the possibility of restoring the troops to the *status quo*, Fort Moultrie being occupied by the Carolinians.

After a few more bitter words the cabinet adjourned. The commissioners called upon the President and presented, in writing, their credentials from the State of South Carolina, empowering them to treat with the general government in regard to the forts, arsenals and other property; but the President would give no recognition to their authority to address him, except as citizens of the United States, and not as commissioners from a foreign power.

At two o'clock, on the afternoon of the 28th, the navy department received a dispatch from Lieutenant James P. Foster, commanding the slaver Bonita, which was carried into Charleston as a prize, that his prisoner, the captain of the Bonita, was taken on a writ of *habeas corpus* before a State judge, who remanded him on the ground of want of jurisdiction; and that while conveying his prisoner from the court to the ship, he was forcibly taken from his custody by a mob.

Mr. Holt, Postmaster General, sent orders to the sub-treasurer, at Charleston, to remit all the balance — thirty-five thousand dollars, on the post-office account — in his possession, immediately, to the credit of that department.

An immense Union meeting was held at Memphis, Tennessee.

On the 31st, Senator Benjamin, of Louisiana, made a

secession speech in the United States Senate. He argued at great length, and with eloquence, to prove that a State has an inherent right to secede, and cannot be coerced. He quoted Webster and Madison, to sustain his position; said all pretexts about collecting the revenue, or enforcing the laws in the seceding States, were but another name for overcoming their objections by war.

He argued that they could not collect the revenue by force; that such threats were only a pretext to cover up the real question, which was this:— Shall we acknowledge the independence of a seceding State, or reduce her to subjection by war? — said he had repeatedly warned the North that they were driving them to a point that would result in a separation, and referred to a speech he made, in 1856, predicting this result, and in which he said the time would come when the South would throw the sword into the scale with all the rights of the South, because he did not believe there could be peaceable secession; that his words then uttered had proved true. He would to God that the fears of civil war, then expressed, would prove only fears; but it seemed almost as if the other side of the chamber desired to bring about a civil war; that South Carolina had declared herself separated from the Union, and that she was not alone, for Mississippi, Alabama, Georgia, Florida, and other Southern States, would soon follow; that the North had caused all this ruin; a sectional President had been elected, who could, with the aid of a sectional Senate, grant all the benefits to and appoint from one section all the officers in the gift of the government, and thus ruin the South; and after enumerating the various indignities heaped upon them by the North, and commenting upon the evils and disadvantages of a connection with the free States, he concluded by saying:—:

"Our committee has reported, this morning, that no possible scheme of adjustment can be devised. The day of adjustment is passed; if you propose to make one now, you are too late. And now, senators, within a very few weeks we part, to meet again in one common council-chamber of the nation no more, forever. We desire, we beseech you, to let this parting be in peace. I conjure you to indulge in no vain delusions that duty, or conscience, or interest, or honor, impose on you the necessity of invading our States, and shedding the blood of our people. You have no possible justification for it. I trust it is from no craven spirit, or any sacrifice of the dignity or honor of my own State, that I make this last appeal, but from far higher and holier motives. If, however, it shall prove vain, if you are resolute to pervert the government, framed by the fathers for the protection of our rights, into an instrument for subjugating and enslaving us, then, appealing to the Supreme Judge of the universe for the rectitude of our intentions, we must meet the issue as best becomes freemen defending all that is dear to man. What may be the fate of this horrible contest, none can foretell. The fortunes of war may be adverse to our arms; you may carry desolation into our peaceful land, and with torch and firebrand may set our cities in flames; you may even emulate the atrocities of those who, in the days of the Revolution, hounded on the blood-thirsty savage; you may give the protection of your advancing armies to the furious fanatics who desire nothing more than to add the horrors of servile insurrection to civil war; you may do all this, and more, but you never can subjugate the free sons of the soil into vassals, paying tribute to your power; you can never degrade them to a servile and inferior race, — never, never."

In the House, Mr. Stevens, of Pennsylvania, offered a resolution calling on the President to state to Congress the exact condition of the public forts and arsenals in South Carolina, and an account of all the arms distributed during the year, etc. etc. This was rejected, and a

substitute by Mr. Stanton, of Ohio, adopted, directing the
military committee to inquire and report how, to whom,
and for what price, arms had been distributed and sold
during the year; also the condition of the forts and
arsenals.

January 2d. Senator Baker, of Oregon, proceeded to
address the Senate, on the crisis, referring first to Mr.
Benjamin's speech as the best he had heard; but it re-
minded him of what had been said of a certain book that
had been written, that it would have been best if it had
never been written at all.

He said the government was a substantial power; its
Constitution a perpetuity, and its power capable of exercise against domestic treason or foreign foes; and referred
to some authorities quoted by Mr. Benjamin, disproving
the latter's arguments.   He acknowledged that " personal liberty bills," if they hindered the operation of the
fugitive slave law, ought to be repealed.

January 2d. Governor Morgan, of New York, in his
message, delivered at the convening of the legislature of
his State, recommended the repeal of the personal liberty
bill, and, also, recommended other States to do the same.

Captain Charles Stone was appointed Inspector General
of Militia in the district of Columbia, at the recommendation of General Scott.

A hundred guns were fired in the Park, at New York,
in honor of the action of Major Anderson. Salutes of
thirty-three guns were fired, in honor of the gallant conduct of Major Anderson, in Boston, Burlington, Vt.,
Philadelphia, Trenton, N. J., Auburn, Schenectady, and
Utica, N. Y.

3d. The demands of the South Carolina commissioners were refused by the President.

4th. The national fast day was generally observed
throughout the States.

Governor Sprague, of Rhode Island, in his proclamation, seconds Mr. Buchanan's idea that we ought to fast and pray, and proposes to "supplicate Almighty God for deliverance from *corrupt rulers;*" imploring that "our laws may be faithfully and fearlessly executed; our Constitution and Union may be preserved, in their original strength and purity; and those who have charge of our national affairs be imbued with sufficient patriotism and courage to maintain the government inviolate, and to uphold the constitutional rights of the people in every section of the country.

January 5th. Steamship Star of the West left New York, with two hundred and fifty artillerists and marines.

8th. Jacob Thompson, Secretary of the Interior, resigned. Thus we receive, in the short space of one month, the resignation of four of the highest officials of the government, and those to whom our country should look in her hours of darkness and peril. General Cass retired disgusted and aggrieved at the inactivity of the President.

Howell Cobb, Secretary of the Treasury, maintained his position until the treasury became bankrupt; then, feeling that the North "violated all her pledges," and that every hour he remained only served to "*degrade him,*" he "*conscientiously*" resigned and left for the South.

John B. Floyd was content with his position, as Secretary of War, until the principal guns and munitions of war had been transferred South, from Northern arsenals, navy yards, etc., a large amount of government property seized, and the South armed and prepared for war; then he "very conscientiously" resigned.

Jacob Thompson remained Secretary of the Interior until the poor "Indian" had been robbed of all his funds, then his "*sense of honor*" compelled him to resign.

4*

CHAPTER III.

Such shapes of earth and time have I not watched
In other years; but calamity methinks
Is creeping nigh, her cruel plot being hatched.

WE give here a little circumstance which goes to show the excitable state of the public mind at that time, and, particularly, in the border States. At Harper's Ferry, Jefferson County, Va., the spot made ever memorable by the bloody John Brown raid, the 7th of January was characterized by the greatest excitement, and warlike preparations were made on a large scale to meet what proved to be only an *imaginary* foe.

It seems that, from some quarter or other, news had come to the Ferry that the government had dispatched a force of United States troops to take possession of the arsenal at the Ferry, and hold it, — its arms, stores, and munitions of war, — in view of the reported march that was to be made by insurgents in the border States on the capitol at Washington. This report threw the Harper's Ferry people, especially the employees at the arsenal, of whom there were between three and four hundred, into a state of the wildest excitement; and straightway the cry arose, "To arms! To arms!" Accordingly, when the express train, which left Baltimore at four in the evening, and arrived at the Ferry about eight, had crossed the Long Bridge and reached the latter place, the passengers were astonished to find some three or four hundred armed men drawn up in battle array, ready to welcome the United States soldiers " with bloody hands to hospitable graves;" or, in other words, waiting to enact a scene

42

before which all the high extravaganzas thus far played
off by South Carolina should pale into utter insignifi-
cance. Fortunately for the peace and the ever after rep-
utation of that part of the country, — and fortunately,
perhaps, for the three hundred men in arms, — there
were no United States troops aboard. None had been
sent, — none, that any one on the train knew of, were expected to .be sent. Some were pleased, and others were
petulant and irritable that they had no chance to show
their valor and courage in opposition to the government,
and their devotion to secessiondom ; and, after discussing
their deeds of " chivalry " which might have been enacted had the troops arrived, they began to dwindle away,
one by one, till finally all were gone, and peace and order
reigned.

January 9. The " Star of the West," an unarmed
steamer bearing re-enforcements to Major Anderson, in
endeavoring to enter the harbor of Charleston, about
daylight in the morning, was fired into by the garrison on
Morris Island, and also by Fort Moultrie, then in command of Major Ripley. The steamer put about and
went to sea, Morris Island battery still firing upon them
until they were out of reach of their guns. Fort Sumter did not respond.

As this intelligence spread on the wings of the telegraph throughout the country, the effect produced upon
the public mind in all quarters was that we were on the
eve of war. The first gun had been fired, and the end
of the struggle no man could foresee. During the forenoon of the same day, Major Anderson dispatched Lieutenant Hall with a flag of truce to Charleston, where he
delivered a communication from the Major to Governor
Pickens, wherein he recapitulates the facts concerning
the Star of the West, and requests to know if the action
of the State troops is authorized ; and says that if such
action is not disclaimed by the South Carolina authori-

ties, he will prevent the passage of all vessels to the city of Charleston.

Governor Pickens replied that the re-enforcement of the fort was regarded as an act of hostility to South Carolina, and that he approved of the attack upon the Star of the West.

After some deliberation, Major Anderson concluded to refer the subject to the federal authorities at Washington, and Lieutenant Talbot was sent to the capitol with dispatches.

January 11. Phillip F. Thomas, of Maryland, Secretary of Treasury, resigned, and Hon. John A. Dix, of New York, appointed in his place.

An abolition meeting at Rochester, N. Y., was broken up Jan. 12. The Star of the West arrived at New York, from Charleston, and, on the thirteenth, landed her troops at Governor's Island.

Senator Seward, of N. Y., made a great Union speech in the United States Senate.

15th. Major-General Sanford tendered the first division N. Y. State Militia, 7000 men, to the Commander-in-Chief, for any service which might be required.

18th. The Massachusetts State Legislature tendered to the President of the United States aid in men and money.

20th. Wendell Phillips, in a speech at Music Hall, Boston, declared himself to be a disunionist, and said he was glad to see the movement of South Carolina.

21st. United States Senators, Jefferson Davis, of Mississippi; Fitzpatrick and Clay, of Alabama; Yulee and Mallory, of Florida; and the whole Alabama and Georgia delegation, formally withdrew from Congress. Postal service in Florida was discontinued.

22d. Sherrard Clemens, of Virginia, made a Union speech in the U. S. House of Representatives.

24th. The annual meeting of the Mass. Anti-Slavery Society, in Boston, was broken up.

25th. The Rhode Island personal liberty bill was repealed by the legislature.

27th. The grand jury for the District of Columbia made presentments of Ex-Secretary Floyd for maladministration in office, complicity in the abstraction of Indian bonds, and conspiring against the government.

31st. The attorney general of South Carolina made proposals to government, in behalf of the State, to buy Fort Sumter.

February 4th. The commissioners to the peace conference, proposed by Virginia, met at Washington. Delegates were present from Virginia, Maryland, Kentucky, Tennessee, North Carolina, New York, Ohio, Missouri, New Jersey, Pennsylvania, Indiana, Illinois, Connecticut, New Hampshire, Vermont, Delaware, Rhode Island, and Massachusetts, — Ex-President Tyler chosen president.

5th. Senators Slidell and Benjamin and the Louisiana delegation withdrew from Congress.

9th. Tennessee voted by a large majority to remain in the Union.

13th. Virginia State convention met at Richmond.

22d. Abraham Lincoln, the President elect, broke up the programme of his route to Washington, and left Harrisburg, Pa., secretly, in a special night train, for Washington, owing to fears of assassination in Baltimore.

The Union celebration in San Francisco on the 22d was universally observed in a style similar to that of the Fourth of July. Business was generally suspended. The Union meeting on that day was attended by 20,000 people. Union speeches were made, and resolutions adopted declaring the unalterable attachment of California to the Union; that there exists no power under the Constitution for a State to secede; that California will cheerfully acquiesce in any honorable plan for the adjustment of the difficulties so as to secure the rights of all the States; that if one or more States should finally separate from the confederacy, California would still cling to the Union; that California repudiates the Pacific republic project; that the true attitude of the people of California is that of fraternal kindness toward all the States, and her honor and interests demand that she should do all in her power to bring about harmony and reunion. The meeting was enthusiastic.

[1] On Wednesday, February 27, Mr. Lincoln was officially welcomed to the capitol by Mayor Berritt and the members of the city council. Mr. Berritt, in addressing the President elect, spoke as follows: —

" Mr. Lincoln: As the President elect under the Constitution of the United States, you are soon to stand in the august presence of a great nation of freemen, and to enter upon the discharge of the duties of the highest public trust known to our form of government, and under circumstances menacing the peace and permanency of the republic, which have no parallel in the history of our country. It is our earnest wish that you may be able, as we have no doubt you will, to perform these duties in such a manner as shall reflect honor to yourself; restore peace and harmony to our now distracted country; and, at last, bring the old ship of state into the harbor of safety and prosperity, thereby deservedly securing the plaudits of a whole world. I avail myself of this occasion to say that the citizens of Washington, true to the instincts of constitutional liberty, will ever be found faithful to all the obligations of patriotism; and as their chief

[1] Some have charged Mr. Lincoln with cowardice in avoiding Baltimore, but it appears to be the fault of Baltimore, not of Mr. Lincoln, for " Mr. Buchanan met with the same difficulty when he left Lancaster, four years before, on his way to Washington, as President elect; he was threatened by the rowdies of Baltimore with personal violence, in any number of anonymous letters, and it made such an impression on him that, in company with a few friends, he took a private carriage, leaving his escort and a dinner that had been prepared for him behind.

magistrate, and in accordance with the honored usage, I bid you welcome to the seat of government."

Mr. Lincoln, in reply, thanked the mayor, and, through him, the municipal authorities of the city, for their kind welcome; and declared it to be the first time in his life, since the present phase of politics had presented itself in this country, that he had spoken publicly within a region of country where the institution of slavery existed; and expressed it as his opinion that very much of the ill-feeling which has existed, and still exists, between the people of the section from whence he came and the people of the slave States was owing to a misunderstanding between each other which unhappily prevails. At the same time assuring the mayor, and all the people present, that he had not at that time, nor ever had, any other than as kindly feelings towards them as to the people of his own section, and that it was not his purpose to withhold from them any of the benefits of the Constitution, under any circumstances, that he would not feel himself constrained to withhold from his own neighbors; and expressed the hope that when they should become better acquainted they would like each other the more; and again thanking them for their kind reception, soon afterwards withdrew.

February 27th. The peace convention adjourned without day, after adopting a plan of adjustment embracing the restoration of the Missouri compromise, a condition respecting the acquisition of new territory which made necessary the concurrence of a majority of Northern and Southern senators, agreeing that there should be no future amendments of the Constitution to allow Congress to interfere with slavery in any State or territory, etc., etc.

February 28th. Senator Crittenden, of Kentucky, presented the recommendations of the peace convention, in the Senate, and favored their adoption.

Mr. Corwin's proposed amendment to the Constitution,

as adopted by the committee of thirty-three, passed the House of Representatives.

March 2d. The new tariff bill signed by President Buchanan.

March 4th. Mr. Corwin's proposed amendment passed the Senate.

The thirty-sixth Congress adjourned, *sine die.*

President Lincoln was inaugurated.

Aside from telegraphic dispatches, received by General Scott and others, cautioning them to be on the lookout for gunpowder plots at the capitol, and anonymous letters with threats of personal violence to the President on the day of his inauguration, with rumors of riotous preparations being made on a large scale, nothing occurred to disturb the tranquillity of the President elect or his friends. These reports, being widely circulated through the public press, brought together at Washington large crowds of people, both political and civil, who were determined that the inauguration should take place, and that the President should be protected at all hazards ; that the people's choice must take his seat at the head of the government of this great nation, let the consequences be what they would. Five hundred special police were detailed for duty on the fourth of March, and soldiers were stationed in the house-tops along the line of procession, to act as sharp-shooters in case of riotous proceedings. The amplest civil and military preparations were made, by the municipal authorities and General Scott, to provide for any emergency which might arise. The day of inauguration, that ever-memorable fourth of March, was ushered in by a most exciting session of the Senate, that body sitting for twelve hours, from seven o'clock the previous evening to seven in the morning ; and as the dial of the clock, that old admonisher of time and things passing away, now told the hour of midnight, and Sunday gave way to Monday, the fourth of March, the Senate chamber presented a curious and animated appearance.   The galleries were crowded to repletion; the ladies' gallery resembling, from the gay dresses of the fair ones there congregated, some gorgeous parterre of flowers; and the gentlemen's gallery seemed one dense black mass of surging, hearing masculines, pushing, struggling and almost clambering over each others' backs in order to get a good look at the proceedings.

The morning broke clear and beautiful, and the hearts of thousands upon thousands of freemen, far and near, beat in rapid succession, and throbbed wildly at the thought of what that day might bring forth, and many, many, with the gray dawn of the morning, wished that day well and peacefully over.   On the floor of the Senate Messrs. Crittenden, Trumbull, Wigfall, Wade, Douglas, and others, kept up a rolling fire of debate, while those not engaged in the discussion betook themselves to the sofas for a comfortable nap during the session, which, it was known, would last all night.   As the morning advanced, the galleries and floor became gradually cleared out, and at eight o'clock only a few remained.   The public buildings, schools, and most places of business, were closed throughout the day; the stars and stripes floated from the City Hall, Capitol, War Department and other public buildings, while not a few of the citizens flung out flags from their houses or across the principal avenues. From early dawn the drum and fife could be heard in every quarter of the city, and the streets were thronged. with the volunteer soldiery, hastening to their respective rendezvous.   Three or four hours elapsed before there was the least chance of entering the Capitol.   Pennsylvania Avenue was thronged with people wending their way to the famous east front.   For four hours the crowd poured on, in one continuous stream of old and young, male and female; staid old Quakers, from Pennsylvania, going to see Friend .Abraham; and lengthy Suckers,

5

Hoosiers and Wolverines, desirous of a peep at Mr. Lincoln; Buckeyes and Yankees, men from California and Oregon, from the north-east and the north-west, and a few from the border States; the large majority, however, were Northern men, there being, apparently, but few Southerners. Previous to the arrival of the procession, the Senate chamber did not present a very animated appearance. The many ladies waiting to see the display did not arrive until late; and the officers, whose gay uniforms and flashing epaulettes relieved so well the sombreness of the national black, were with the Presidential cortege, during the passing of the procession to Willard's Hotel and the march thence to the Capitol.

At five minutes to twelve o'clock, Vice-President Breckenridge and Senator Foote, of the committee of arrangements, entered the Senate chamber escorting the Vice-President elect, Hon. Hannibal Hamlin, whom they conducted to a seat immediately to the left of the chair of the President of the Senate. As the hands of the clock pointed to the hour of twelve the hammer fell, and the second session of the thirty-sixth Congress came to an end. Mr. Breckenridge announced the Senate adjourned without day, and left the chair, to which he immediately conducted Vice-President Hamlin. The foreign diplomatic corps also entered the chamber at the same moment, occupying seats to the right of the chair. It was a subject of general remark that the foreign corps never were so fully represented as on this occasion. The ministers, attachés and others, numbered, in all, above fifty; and their brilliancy of dress, the number of their decorations, crapes, &c., added much to the imposing nature of the scene. Some of the court uniforms were particularly gorgeous, and attracted much attention. The attendance of senators was unusually full, the only absences noticed being those of Messrs. Mason and Hunter of Virginia. At fifteen minutes to one o'clock the judges of the Supreme

Court of the United States were announced by the door-keeper of the Senate. On their entrance all on the floor arose, and the venerable judges, headed by Chief Justice Taney, moved slowly across to the seats assigned them, immediately to the right of the Vice-President, each exchanging salutes with that officer in passing the chair. At ten minutes after one o'clock an unusual stir occurred in the chamber, and the rumor spread like wildfire that the President elect was in the building. At fifteen minutes past one o'clock the marshal and chief, Major B. B. French, entered the chamber, ushering in the President and President elect. They had entered together from the street through a private covered passage-way, on the north side of the Capitol, police officers being in attendance to prevent outsiders from crowding after them. The line of procession was then formed, as follows : — Marshal of the District of Columbia, judges of the Supreme Court and sergeant-at-arms, Senate commitee of arrangements, President of the United States and President elect, Vice-President, Secretary of the Senate, senators, diplomatic corps, heads of the departments, governors and others in the chambers. When the word was given for members of the House to fall into the line of procession a violent rush was made for the door, accompanied by loud outcries, violent pushing and great disturbance. After the procession had reached the platform, Senator Baker, of Oregon, introduced Mr. Lincoln to the assembly. On Mr. Lincoln's advancing to the stand he was cheered, but not very loudly. Unfolding his manuscript, in a loud, clear voice he read his message. During the delivery of the inaugural, which began at half-past one o'clock, Mr. Lincoln was much cheered, especially at any allusion to the Union.

President Buchanan and Chief Justice Taney listened with the utmost attention to every word of the address, and, at its conclusion, the latter administered the usual oath, in answering to which Mr. Lincoln was vociferously cheered. The present inauguration is the eighth ceremony of the kind at which Chief Justice Taney has officiated, having administered the oath of office, successively, to Presidents Van Buren, Tyler, Polk, Taylor, Fillmore, Pierce, Buchanan and Lincoln. The ceremony was exceedingly impressive. The Chief Justice seemed to be very much agitated, and his hands shook very perceptibly with emotion. At the conclusion of the ceremonies the President was escorted to the Senate chamber, thence to his carriage, and the military, forming as in the procession of the morning, accompanied him, with the committee of arrangements, to the White House. On reaching the executive mansion the troops formed in double line, on Maine Avenue, and the barouche containing the Presidential party passed through to the White House. Mr. Buchanan accompanied Mr. Lincoln to the main hall, and there took a farewell leave of him, expressing a hope, in cordial terms, that his administration might prove a happy and a prosperous one. The ex-President then retired. On the arrival of the procession at the White House the marshals were successively introduced to Mr. Lincoln, and then, the line being formed, the rush of people to congratulate the new President was exceedingly great. Thus ended, for the day-time, the inaugural ceremonies.

Though the enthusiasm did not equal that manifested on former occasions, everything passed off quietly. The most ample civil and military preparations were made, by the municipal authorities and General Scott, to provide for any emergency that might arise. The various bodies of United States troops at Washington were stationed in different parts of the city, the sappers and miners alone being in the procession. General Scott, it is said, was near the Capitol, with Capt. Barry's company of artillery and Major Harkin's command, acting as infantry. Officers reported continually, passing to and fro, and it is said the General was heard to exclaim, — "Everything is going on peaceably ; thank God Almighty for it!" During the day military patrols were on duty all over the city, and the greatest vigilance was enjoined upon and observed by the regulars.

The display of soldiery in the procession was very fine, but not equal to the 22d of February. The companies were quite numerous, but of small size. As a rule the Republican associations were placed in the order of march immediately after the ex-President. These organizations had with them a kind of triumphal car, drawn by four white horses, each of which was covered with white cloth on which was the word "Union" in large letters on one side, and the word "Constitution" on the other. The car was decorated with miniature flags, and white, red and blue drapery, and contained thirty-four little girls, representing the States, and two young ladies, respectively representing the North and the South. The whole affair was under the charge of ten Wide-Awakes, in full uniform. Five hundred delegates from New York marched in the procession, four abreast. Several other large delegations also joined the line.

The scene from the east front was very fine. The avenue in front of the portico was thronged with people, the crowd extending a great distance on either side, and reaching far into the Capitol grounds. Every available spot was black with human beings ; boys and men clinging to rails, and mounting on fences, and climbing trees, until they bent beneath their weight. On the outer edge of the concourse, the volunteer soldiery stood at rest during the delivery of the inaugural. A great number of flags were flying, and as the sun shone brightly on the gay dresses of the ladies, and the uniforms and glittering weapons of the soldiery, the scene was exceedingly animated.

5*

It is not my purpose, at this time, to give in detail the inaugural address of President Lincoln, or enter into the minutiæ of that official document as a whole, but only that part of it which pertains to our affairs with the South and treats on the alleged causes of secession, which I copy verbatim.

Extracts from the inaugural address of President Lincoln, delivered March 4th, 1861 : —

"Fellow-Citizens of the United States : — In compliance with a custom as old as the government itself I appear before you to address you briefly, and to take, in your presence, the oath prescribed by the Constitution of the United States, to be taken by the President before he enters on the execution of the duties of his office. I do not consider it necessary, at present, for me to discuss those matters of administration about which there is no special anxiety or excitement. Apprehension seems to exist among the people of the Southern States that, by the accession of a Republican administration, their property and their permanent peace and security are to be endangered. There has never been any reasonable cause for such apprehension. Indeed, the most ample evidence to the contrary has all the while existed, and been open to their inspection. It is found in nearly all the published speeches of him who now addresses you. I do but quote from one of those speeches when I declare that I have no purpose, directly or indirectly, to interfere with the institution of slavery in the States where it now exists. I believe I have no lawful right to do so, and I have no inclination to do so. Those who nominated and elected me did so with full knowledge that I had made this and many similar declarations, and had never recanted them ; and, more than this, they placed in the platform for my acceptance, and as a law to themselves and to me, the clear and emphatic resolution which I now read : —

"'Resolved, That the maintenance inviolate of the rights

of the States, and especially the right of each State to
order and control its own domestic institutions according
to its own judgment exclusively, is essential to that balance of power on which the perfection and endurance of
our political fabric depend ; and we denounce the lawless
invasion, by an armed force, of any State or territory, no
matter under what pretext, as the greatest of crimes.'

" I now reiterate these sentiments, and in doing so I
only press upon the public attention the most conclusive
evidence of which the case is susceptible, that the property, peace and security of no section are to be in any
wise endangered by the now incoming administration.   I
add, too, that all the protection which, consistently with
the Constitution and laws, can be given, will be cheerfully
given to all the States, when lawfully demanded, for
whatever cause, as cheerfully to one section as to another.
There is much controversy about the delivering up of
fugitives from service or labor.   The clause I now read
is as plainly written in the Constitution as any other of its
provisions : —

" ' No person held to service or labor in one State, under
the laws thereof, escaping into another, shall in couse-
quence of any law or regulation therein be discharged
from such service or labor, but shall be delivered up on
claim of the party to whom such service or labor may be
due.'

" It is scarcely questioned that this provision was intended by those who made it for the reclaiming of what we
call fugitive slaves ; and the intention of the law-givers is
the law.   All members of Congress swear their support
to the whole Constitution, — to this provision as much
as any other.   To the proposition, then, that slaves
whose cases come within the terms of this clause shall be
delivered up, their oaths are unanimous.   Now if they
would make the effort, in good temper, would they not, with
equal unanimity, frame and pass a law by means of which

to keep good that unanimous oath ? There is some difference of opinion whether this clause should be enforced by
national or State authority ; but, surely, that difference is
not a very material one. If the slave is to be surrendered,
it can be of but little consequence, to him or to others,
by what authority it is done ; and should any one, in any
case, be content that his oaths should go unkept, on a
merely unsubstantial controversy as to how it shall be
kept ?

" Again, in any law upon this subject, ought not all the
safeguards of liberty, known in civilized and humane ju-
risprudence, to be introduced, so that a free man be not in
any case surrendered as a slave ; and might it not be well,
at the same time, to provide by law for the enforcement
of that clause in the Constitution which guarantees that
the citizens of each State shall be entitled to all the privileges and immunities of citizens in the several States?
I take the official oath, to-day, with no mental reserva-
tions, and with no purpose to control the Constitution or
laws by any hypercritical rules; and, while I do not
choose now to specify particular acts of Congress as
proper to be enforced, I do suggest that it will be much
safer for all, both in official and private stations, to con-
form to and abide by all those acts that stand unrepealed,
than to violate any of them trusting to find impunity in
having them held to be unconstitutional.

" It is seventy-two years since the first inauguration of a
President under our national Constitution. During that
period fifteen different and greatly distinguished citizens
have, in succession, administered the executive branch
of government. They have conducted it through many
perils, and generally with great success; yet with all this
scope for precedent, I now enter upon the same task, for
the brief constitutional term of four years, under grave
and peculiar difficulties.

" A disruption of the federal Union, heretofore only

menaced, is now formidably attempted. I hold that, in contemplation of universal law and of the Constitution, the Union of these States is perpetual. Perpetuity is implied, if not expressed, in the fundamental law of all national governments; it is safe to assert that no government proper ever had a provision in its organic law for its own termination. Continue to execute all the express provisions of our national Constitution, and the Union will endure forever, it being impossible to destroy it except by some action not provided for in the instrument itself.

"Again, if the United States be not a government proper, but an association of States, in the nature of a compact merely, can it as a compact be peaceably unmade, by less than all the parties who made it? One party to a compact may violate it, break it, so to speak, but does it not require all to lawfully rescind it? Descending from these general principles, we find the proposition, that in legal contemplation the Union is perpetual, confirmed by the history of the Union itself. The Union is much older than the Constitution; it was formed, in fact, by the articles of association, in 1774; it was matured and continned by the Declaration of Independence in 1776; it was further matured, and the faith of all the then thirteen States expressly plighted and engaged that it should be perpetual, by the Articles of Confederation in 1778, and, finally, in 1789.

"One of the declared objects for ordaining and establishing the Constitution was to form a more perfect Union; but if destruction by one, or by a part only, of the States be lawfully possible, the Union is less than before the Constitution, having lost the vital element of perpetuity. It follows from these views that no State, upon its own mere motion, can lawfully get out of the Union; that resolves or ordinances to that effect are legally void, and that acts of violence, within any State or States, against

the authority of the United States, are insurrectionary or
revolutionary, according to circumstances. I therefore
consider that, in view of the Constitution and the laws,
the Union is unbroken; and to the extent of my ability
I shall take care, as the Constitution itself expressly enjoins
upon me, that the laws of the Union be faithfully executed in all the States. Doing this I deem to be only a
simple duty on my part, and shall perform it so far as
practicable, unless my rightful masters, the American
people, shall withdraw the requisition, or in some author-
itative manner direct the contrary. I trust this will not
be regarded as a menace, but only as the declared purpose of the Union, that it will constitutionally defend
and maintain itself. In doing this there needs to be no
bloodshed or violence, and there shall be none, unless it
be forced upon the national authority.

"The power confided to me will be used to hold, occupy
and possess the property and places belonging to the government, and collect the duties and imposts; but, beyond
what may be necessary for these objects, there will be no
invasion, no urging of force against or among the people,
anywhere. Where hostility to the United States, in any
interior territory, shall be so great and so universal as to
prevent the competent resident citizens from holding the
federal offices, there will be no attempt to force obnoxious
strangers among people that object. While the strict
legal right may exist for the government to enforce the
exercise of those offices, the attempt to do so would be so
irritating, and so nearly impracticable withal, that I deem
it better to forego, for the time, the uses of such offices.

"The mails, unless repelled, will continue to be furnished
in all parts of the Union, so far as possible. The people,
everywhere, shall have that sense of perfect security which
is most favorable to calm thought and reflection. The
course here indicated will be followed, unless current
events and experience shall show a modification or change

to be proper, and in every case and exigency my best discretion will be exercised, according to circumstances actually existing; and with a view and a hope to a peaceful solution of the national trouble and the restoration of fraternal sympathies and affections.

" That there are persons, in one section or another, who seek to destroy the Union at all events, and are glad of any pretext to do it, I will neither affirm nor deny; but if there should be such I need address no word to them. To those, however, who really love the Union, may I not speak? Before entering upon so grave a matter as the destruction of our national fabric, with all its benefits, its memories and its hopes, would it not be well to ascertain precisely why we do it? Will you hazard so desperate a step, while there is any possibility that any portion of the ills that you fly from have no real existence? Will you, while the certain ills you fly to are greater than all the real ills you fly from, will you risk the commission of so fearful a mistake?

"All profess to be content in the Union if all constitutional rights can be maintained. Is it true, then, that any right plainly written in the Constitution has been denied? I think not. Happily the human mind is so constituted that no party can reach the audacity of doing this. Think, if you can, of a single instance in which a plainly-written provision of the Constitution has ever been denied.

" One section of our country believes slavery is right, and ought to be extended, while the other believes it is wrong and ought not to be extended; this is the only substantial dispute. The fugitive slave clause of the Constitution, and the law for the suppression of the foreign slave-trade, are each as well enforced, perhaps, as any law can ever be in a community where the moral sense of the people imperfectly supports the law itself. The great body of the people abide by the dry legal obligation in both cases, and a few break over in each. This, I think, cannot be perfectly cured, and it would be worse, in both cases, after the separation of the sections, than before. The foreign slave-trade, now imperfectly suppressed, would be ultimately revived without restriction in one section, while fugitive slaves, now only partially surrendered, would not be surrendered at all by the other. Physically speaking, we cannot separate; we cannot remove our respective sections from each other, nor build an impassable wall between them. A husband and wife may be divorced and go out of the presence and beyond the reach of each other; but the different parties of our country cannot do this. They cannot but remain face to face, and intercourse — either amiable or hostile relations — must continue between them. Is it possible, then, to make that intercourse more advantageous or more satisfactory after separation than before? Can aliens make treaties easier than friends can make laws? Can treaties be more faithfully enforced between aliens than laws among friends? Suppose you go to war, you cannot fight always; and when, after much loss on both sides and no gain on either, you cease fighting, the identical questions, as to terms of intercourse, are again upon you.

" This country, with its institutions, belongs to the people who inhabit it. Whenever they shall grow weary of the existing government they can exercise their constitutional right of amending, or their revolutionary right to dismember or overthrow it. I cannot be ignorant of the fact that many worthy and patriotic citizens are desirous of having the national Constitution amended. While I make no recommendation of amendment, I fully recognize the authority of the people over the whole subject, to be exercised in either of the modes prescribed in the instrument itself; and I should, under existing circumstances, favor rather than oppose a fair opportunity being offered the people to act upon it.

" I will venture to add that, to me, the convention mode seems preferable, in that it allows amendments to originate with the people themselves, instead of only permitting them to take a proposition originated by others, not especially chosen for the purpose, and which might not be precisely such as they would wish to either accept or refuse.

" I understand a proposed amendment to the Constitution, which amendment I have not seen, has passed Congress, to the effect that the federal government shall never interfere with the domestic institutions of the States, including that of persons held to service. To avoid misconstruction of what I have said, I depart from my purpose not to speak of particular amendments so far as to say, that, holding such a provision to be now implied constitutional law, I have no objection to its being made express and irrevocable.

" The chief magistrate derives all his authority from the people, and they have conferred none upon him to fix terms for the separation of the States ; the people themselves can do this alone, if they choose, but the Executive, as such, has nothing to do with it. His duty is to administer the present government, as it came to his hands, and to transmit it unimpaired by him to his successor.

" Why should there not be a patient confidence in the ultimate justice of the people ? Is there any better or equal hope in the world ? In our present differences is either party without faith of being right ? If the Almighty Ruler of Nations, with his eternal truth and justice, be on your side of the North, or on yours of the South, that truth and that justice will surely prevail, by the judgment of this great tribunal — the American people.

" By the frame of government under which we live, the same people have wisely given their public servants but little power for mischief, and have, with equal wisdom,

6

provided for the return of that little to their own hands, at very short intervals. While the people retain virtue and vigilance, no administration of any extreme of wickedness or folly can very seriously injure the government in the short space of four years.

"My countrymen, one and all; think calmly and well upon this whole subject. Nothing valuable can be lost by taking time. If there be an object to hurry any of you, in hot haste, to a step which you would never take deliberately, that object will be frustrated by taking time; but no good object can be frustrated by it. Such of you as are now dissatisfied still have the old Constitution unimpaired, and, on the sensitive point, the laws of your own framing under it; while the new administration have no immediate power, if it would, to change either. If it were admitted that you who are dissatisfied hold the right side in the dispute, there is still no single good cause for precipitate action.

"Intelligence, patriotism, Christianity and a firm reliance on Him who has never yet forsaken this favored land, are still competent to adjust, in the best way, all our present difficulties. In your hands, my dissatisfied fellow-countrymen, and not in mine, is the momentous issue of civil war. The government will not assail you. You can have no conflict without being yourselves the aggressors. You have no oath registered in heaven to destroy the government, while I shall have the most solemn one to preserve, protect and defend it.

"I am loth to close; we are not enemies, but friends; we must not be enemies. Though passion may have strained, it must not break our bonds of affection. The mystic chords of memory, stretching from every battle-field and patriot grave to every living heart and hearth-stone, all over this broad land, will yet swell the chorus of the Union when again touched, as surely they will be, by the better angels of our nature."

Mr. Lincoln's delivery was good, with but little gesture and small pretence of oratory, yet it fell upon the ear like right words, well spoken; and as he uttered the closing sentence of the address, a loud and still louder and more prolonged cheer announced that the inaugural was delivered, and the long, fearful struggle was over, and a republican President safely inaugurated; and not even with the close of the ceremony did the curious cease to speculate as to the probabilities and chances of his assassination, which was confidently expected, though of course greatly to be dreaded, followed as it would be by riot, panic, and an immediate necessity for a display of force.

But that brave old veteran, General Scott, was prepared for any emergency, and three minutes would have found artillery, cavalry and infantry ready at their posts to put down insurrection and protect the national capital, at all hazards. But the day passed off peaceably, and no foul deed was done to stain our country's honor.

Mr. Lincoln, on being asked whether he felt at all frightened while delivering his inaugural address, the threats of assassination having been so numerous, replied that he had no such sensation, and that he had often experienced much greater fear in addressing a dozen Western men on the subject of temperance.

The delivery of the message commenced at 1.30 P. M., and at four o'clock it had been telegraphed to all the principal cities, and was in the hands of all the agents of the associated press.

The inaugural of President Lincoln met with very general commendation throughout the free States. The journals that give voice to the popular feeling praise the candor, ability, and firm yet conciliatory spirit, of the address, while a few papers, politically opposed to the President, condemn, though faintly, its leading features. But he will be sustained by the great mass of the people, whose sentiments he has so truly reflected. In speaking of the address, a Providence paper contains the following brief paragraph : —

" His honest, simple, straight-forward declarations of fidelity to the spirit of our government and Constitution must commend themselves to all, and awaken a response in every patriotic heart. No language could be chosen which would more strongly and unequivocally express the resolve to respect the rights of the South, to let slavery in the States utterly alone, to fulfil the constitutional obligation respecting fugitive slaves, and to treat with the utmost kindness the citizens of the Southern States, than that which the President employs."

And, again, a Newburyport paper says : — " President Lincoln's inaugural will be read by all. It will be admired by every patriot in the land. It is a glorious message — words of wisdom, of conciliation, of peace; yes, and as brave and firm as pacific. It has about it nothing noisy, declamatory and boisterous; it bears upon its every line the calmness of self-reliant truth, and it carries with it a consciousness of strength that can afford to bear and forbear, and yet possess the power, when necessary, to assert and maintain the right."

March 22d. Dr. Fox, of the navy, visited Major Anderson, as a special messenger of government.

March 25th. Col. Lamon, government messenger, had an interview with Governor Pickens and General Beauregard.

April 3d. Long cabinet meeting on Fort Sumter business. Great activity in the navy department.

We have thus far, the reader will see, given only the Northern side of the question; we now propose to retrace our steps and give an account of the movements in the Southern States during the same period,— thinking this mode preferable, as the commingling of events would distract our readers, and cause them to partially lose sight of the chain of proceedings on either side.

CHAPTER IV.

In vain is the strife : when its fury is past,
Their fortunes must flow in one channel at last,
As the torrents that rush from the mountains of snow
Roll, mingled in peace, through the valleys below.
ATLANTIC MONTHLY.

NOTHING can be more absurd than the claim that the success of the Republican party has brought about the present condition of affairs at the South. That the wickedness, incompetency and inability of the last administration constitute one of the principal causes of the existing national troubles and peril, is evident enough to all honest-minded and intelligent citizens; and that the President of the United States, especially, has been weighed in the balance and found wanting, is a truth *mournfully* obvions to the whole people of the land.

The fire-eaters at the South have contributed their full share towards the mischief. The Rhetts of South Carolina, and the Wendell Phillipses of Boston, who regard the Union as " a league with hell and a covenant with death," can boast that they have " *labored faithfully for twenty years* " to dissever the bonds which fasten together our glorious Union. The Greeleys, John Browns, and others of the Beecher school have contributed their mite towards discord and disunion, while the reverend Beecher and other electioneering parsons, who prostitute the pulpit to partisan politics, and use the influence which belongs to ministers of the gospel for political purposes, have constantly fanned the flame, and kept it alive, which might ere this, if left to itself, have become extinct.

When, in these Northern States, we enter the church dedicated to Almighty God, where we expect to hear preached Christ and him crucified, " peace on earth and good-will to men," we find the pulpit has been prostituted for the purpose of enlisting its adherents and hearers in this antislavery crusade against the South, as a part and parcel of its religious teachings, berating and condemning our Southern brethren because they happen to be born in a land where there exists an institution which they themselves had no hand in establishing.

The prevailing idea entertained by most of the leading statesmen, at the time of the formation of the Constitution, was that the enslavement of the African was in violation of the laws of nature. It was an evil they knew not well how to deal with; but the general opinion of the men of that day was, that somehow or other, in the order of Providence, the institution would be evanescent, and pass away.

Much has been said and written, by the extremists of the abolition party, which has served to inflame the hot blood of the South, who receive it, and without investigation charge it upon the North, as the ruling sentiment of the people; yet, notwithstanding, the oft-repeated assertion of the South, of injuries received and wrongs perpetrated, is a mere fallacy to assist in the work of disunion.

The *real work* has been accomplished by temporizing politicians, who have sought for momentary local success in catering to a deluded populace, but have falsely calculated upon being able to control the storm ere it should prove destructive. While we would condemn the course pursued by Northern politicians and ultra abolitionists, for their aggressions on slavery, we see no just or reasonable cause for the action of the South, or why fears need be entertained for their constitutional rights.

The Vice-President of the Confederate States, Mr. A.

H. Stevens, in a speech made at Savannah, March 21st, 1861, says: —

"The Constitution, it is true, secures every essential guarantee to the institution (slavery) while it should last, and hence no argument can be justly used against the constitutional guarantees thus secured, because of the common sentiment of the day."

The secession movement, which took form and consistency by the action of South Carolina immediately after the election of Lincoln, was not the conception of an hour; it was not the result of the election of a Republican President; it was not that the Constitution gave them no rights, or equality in the Union; it was not the result of wrongs inflicted upon the South by the free States; nor was it the agitation of the slavery question, which have brought upon us the horrors of fratricidal war. The prime moving cause is ambition, — the hungering and thirsting after the balance of power; — that sordid ambition which would prompt them to force their way into the highest positions of power, even though it lay over heaps of the slain and through seas of blood, and then weep, like Alexander, because they had not another world to conquer.

This is the pervading spirit of Southern partisan leaders, who would, Judas-like, sell their country for filthy lucre; yet their keen perceptive faculties told them they must have an excuse, and in order to give the rebellion a semblance of justice they made the slavery question their pretence; and the election of Lincoln, with his Republican principles, afforded them a single thread on which to suspend their operations.

In 1850, when the slavery question was agitated, and trouble was anticipated therefrom, a gentleman from Boston asked General Houston how it could be settled. The General replied,— "You go North and shoot six men, and I will go South and shoot half-a-dozen, then, I think, things will go on quietly."

The love of the Union was so strong in the majority of Southern hearts, the disinclination to encounter the hazards of a revolution so apparent, it became necessary for the leaders to act with great caution in setting on foot their movement for disunion. If the people demurred, they were told by the immediate secessionists that the North had pursued, from the inception of the government up to the present time, one continual course of aggression, — that they had no equality in the Union, in fact that they were but the slaves of the North; until, in listening to the inflammatory appeals of their speakers, they could, in imagination, *almost* hear the clanking of Northern chains around them. The old story was told, of wrongs endured, of slaves stolen, of unjust imposition of taxes by way of tariff levies, of unconstitutional personal liberty bills; then*the evident fact that the institution of slavery was to be excluded from the territories in the West, thus seemingly denying the South of what they called their rights in that unsettled domain; then, as the topmost " crowning stone " of all the indignities heaped upon them, the North had become so heartless and so estranged as to elect a " sectional President," which they considered a sufficient reason to justify them, in the eyes of the civilized world, for secession;—though a mere pretence, as will be seen by the declaration of the leading spirits of the South Carolina convention (as quoted by Governor Hicks in his address to the people of Maryland), that neither the election of Lincoln, nor the non-execution of the fugitive slave law, nor both combined, constitute their grievances; that the real cause of their discontent dates as far back as 1833.

In 1858 the leaders of the rebellion began to prepare the minds of the people for *immediate* secession. In the fall of that year, Jefferson Davis, in a speech at Jackson, Mississippi, took the position of a direct secession advocate. He says,—" If an abolitionist be chosen President of the United States, you will have presented to you the question of whether you will permit the government to pass into the hands of your avowed and implacable enemies; that such a result would be a species of revolution, by which the purposes of the government would be destroyed, and the observance of its forms entitled to no respect;" and intimated that, in that event, it was their duty to provide for their safety outside of the Union, declaring that, otherwise, they would be deprived of their birthright, and reduced to a state worse than the colonial dependence of their fathers.

This catalogue of indignities and fallacies, when properly presented to the excitable and sensitive people of the South, met with a hearty response. It was too much for them to bear. They agreed upon the matter of grievance, and resolved to maintain their right to a separate confedcracy at the point of the sword; and the election of an " abolitionist," that is, any man with Northern or free-soil principles, was to be the signal for an effort to cast off allegiance to the Constitution.

The South felt that more territory must be had at any sacrifice. Kansas and Nebraska lost, all was lost, — Henry Clay's " Compromise Act " of 1821 guaranteeing to all that region freedom forever, and Texas could not for years gain population sufficient to allow of her subdivision into States.

The compromise consisted of admitting Missouri as a slave State, but conceding, as an equivalent for Northern concession in· the premises, the prohibition of any further slave territory north of the parallel 36 degrees 30 minutes. The compromise, though unpalatable to the opponents of the right of slave extension, was accepted as a solemn guarantee against all further extension. Had it not been proposed and pledged as such a guarantee, the bill of Mr. Clay never could have passed the House·of Representatives.

It was not until August, 1821, that the State was admitted, which, together with the later admission of Arkansas and Florida, confirmed the supremacy of the South in the national councils; a supremacy which was not disturbed until the 4th of January, 1854, when Mr. Douglas, chairman of the committee on territories, in the United States Senate, introduced a bill for the organization of the territories of Kansas and Nebraska, which provided that the said territory, or any portion of the same, when admitted as a State, shall be received into the Union with or without slavery, as their constitution may prescribe at the time of their admission;—thus abrogating the venerable and respected Missouri Compromise Act of 1821, and giving to the people of a territory the right to make their own laws,—denying to Congress the power to legislate laws for its territories.

That act became a law, after one of the most exciting sessions of Congress known for many years; and it proved to be one of the most fatal acts for the peace of the country which could have been conceived. It alarmed the North; from the South came armed bands who pursued the anti-slavery settlers in the territories with a vengeance, making the record of 1855 and '56 one of outrage and bloodshed.

The North, aggravated by this armed attempt to make a slave State out of soil unfitted for slave labor, poured in its settlers, armed them for defence, gave them supplies to sustain them through the day of trial, and, eventually, obtained the victory through the action of the principle of "Squatter Sovereignty," and obtained control of affairs by mere force of numbers.

The struggle to make Kansas a free State called into existence the Republican party, which, in a brief period, elected its candidate to the chief magistracy.

Mortified at their defeat, cut off from any further extension of slave representation, the Southern States saw before them their long-apprehended disaster of a minority in the government. If they remained in the Union, it must be as the weaker half. At this their pride revolted. The "balance of power" ranks were weakened by the election of a Republican President, as it closed up the avenues to the accession of more slave territory. In this way, and in no other, can it be said that the election of Lincoln precipitated this rebellion.

Had the South succeeded in electing their candidate to the Presidency, who would administer the government after the pattern of the last administration, grant all their requests in the way of rebuilding their forts, strengthening their fortifications, providing them with military stores, arms and munitions of war, then, undoubtedly, rebellion and all its train of blood would have been averted until the next Presidential election, as it would give them an additional four years to prepare for the conflict which must eventually come. It is urged by the immediate leaders of the secession movement that the North had perverted the Constitution from its original intent and purposes, that they had no equality in the Union, and no hopes of redress for grievances, only in secession.

We would say, for the benefit of those who make the plea that the South has been denied her rights and just share in the government, that for sixty-four years out of seventy-two the executive chair has been filled nearly all the time by Southern Presidents, or, when not by Southern men, by those possessing the confidence of the South; and of all the offices in the gift of the government, in every department, far more than her proportionate share has always been enjoyed by the South; that our army and navy have for years been controlled by Southern men; that our ships of war, and the fortifications along our coast, have nearly all been officered and commanded by men of Southern principles, to the exclusion of the sons of the North.

Then, again, the right of free speech has been asserted by Southern senators, in the halls of Congress, who claim the privilege of expressing their opinions freely on all subjects, even to vilifying opposite parties in unmeasured terms; but when a Northern senator acts upon the same principle, and speaks according to the dictates of his own conscience, he must apologize, or is visited summarily with the cane or the challenge.

New York alone has nearly double the free population of the six original "seceded States," yet she had only thirty-three representatives to their twenty-six; which proves how largely slaves are represented in Congress,— the negroes entering into "population" in the proportion of five negroes for three in count, thus bearing to Congress the preponderating weight of their votes without any of the rights of citizenship appertaining to them.

And, again, Ohio has more free white population than the whole six States originally seceded, yet she had only twenty-one representatives in Congress, while they had twenty-six.

Whether these facts prove that the South has been denied her rights, we leave our readers to judge; and how far the South stands acquitted before the tribunal of nations and the bar of justice, time, and the succeeding pages of this work, will show.

It is not necessary to the accomplishment of our purpose (giving a history of the rebellion) to go farther back than the Presidential election, as we have touched, though lightly, on former feuds; and the feeling of prejudice which has existed between the two sections, for many years, is well known to our readers, and requires no comment.

We find, under date Richmond, Va., October 31, 1860, that war preparations were commenced, that arms and ammunitions were being rapidly distributed, and a determination to resist the general government was developing more and more each day. They regarded the Union as founded upon a very uncertain basis, and that, in case of Lincoln's election, the long-threatened crash must soon come, and all were busy preparing for it.

Senator Wigfall, of Texas notoriety, in a speech at Huntsville, Alabama, took occasion to say,—"I would see the Union rent in a thousand fragments before I would vote for John Bell."

November 5th. The legislature of South Carolina met at Columbia, and received the Governor's (Gist's) message. Therein he suggested immediate secession, in case Lincoln was elected, and earnestly recommended military re-organization, and that every man in the State, between the ages of eighteen and forty-five, should be armed by the State with the most efficient weapons of modern warfare, and also recommended raising, without delay, ten thousand volunteers, to be in readiness at the shortest notice, and adds, "that they may trust their cause to the Supreme Disposer of events." An immense crowd assembled in the evening, at the Congaree House, and serenaded Senator Chesnut, who made a long and eloquent speech, declaring the last hope of the Union gone, and resistance unavoidable.

At the celebration in Savannah, of the completion of the Charleston and Savannah railroad, the mayor pledged fifty thousand Georgians to rush to the assistance of South Carolina, if coerced; Collector Colcock, of Charleston, made an eloquent disunion speech; Mr. Buchanan was toasted as "the last of an illustrious line;" the greatest enthusiasm for a Southern Confederacy prevailed, and all were resolved to fight.

Same day, at Portsmouth, Va., Governor Wise made a disunion speech of over four hours in length. He protested that he would never submit to Lincoln's election. He closed amid the wildest enthusiasm. For several minutes the house shook with the shouts of the excited multitude.

7

November 6.   Presidential election day.   The news of the Republican triumph was received throughout the Southern States with loud demonstrations of civil war and disunion.

On the 8th a mass meeting of the citizens was held at Savannah to consider the result of the election, at which it was unanimously resolved, that the election of Lincoln and Hamlin ought not, and would not be submitted to, and suggested to the legislature to take steps to organize and arm the military forces of the State.   A Southern Rights club hoisted a banner in one of the public squares, with this inscription, —

EQUALITY OF THE STATES,

the painting of a rattlesnake, with the motto, —

DON'T TREAD ON ME;

and though but forty-eight hours since the reception of the news of Lincoln's election, the feeling of the people was clearly manifested by the cheers that greeted the appearance of the banner; minute-men were organizing, and old men and young were mounting the secession badge, — a blue cockade.

In Macon, Ga., and Mobile, Ala., the excitement was intense, and corps of minute-men were organizing.

A correspondent writing from Columbia, S. C., and Charleston, under date Nov. 9, says, "There is no need of speeches to inflame the people; they are, to a man, for secession;" and gives an account of the furore of excitement created by the resignation of the officers of the United States Court in that city.   It was estimated that at least five thousand people called to pay their respects to ex-Judge Magrath.   He addressed them in glowing words as to the great responsibilities and demands of the crisis, and they manifested the most profound emotions by continually-recurring applause.   Till nearly midnight the streets presented the most animated appearance. The crowd illuminated their passage by rockets and other fireworks, and the air resounded with their deafening cries.

November 10. Senator Chesnut, of South Carolina, resigned his seat in the United States Senate. A bill was introduced in the South Carolina legislature to call out and equip ten thousand volunteers, and ordered an election of delegates to a convention to take action on the question of secession, the election to be held Dec. 6, the convention to assemble Dec. 17. The legislature appointed the 21st instant as a day of fasting, humiliation and prayer.

In the evening a great crowd, numbering about two thousand persons, assembled in front of the Congaree House, Columbia, S. C., and were addressed by Judge Magrath, Messrs. Connor, Colcock, and Cunningham. Mr. Magrath said South Carolina had a right to secede. The people, the legislature and Heaven will say she has the right; and if the government at Washington should say she has not the right, then let the government prove it by taking the right away.

Mr. Colcock said that, although this was a large meeting, he wished to see one more in it, and that was Abraham Lincoln. He would take him by the hand and bring him to the platform, and tell him to look upon that great crowd, and then ask him if he ever expected to wave his presidential sceptre over the heads of that people. "Honest Abe," he knew, with downcast eyes, would answer, "Never."

Immense excitement throughout the South. Large meetings held in New Orleans, Augusta, Montgomery and Vicksburg, to favor disunion. Great numbers of resignations of postmasters, custom-house officers, etc., received at the departments at Washington. "Minute-men" organizations making throughout the cotton States.

November 11. Senator Hammond, of South Carolina, resigned his seat in the United States Senate.

In Charleston, on the 12th, at night, a large and enthusiastic meeting was held at Institute Hall. The galleries were filled with ladies, and every part of the building was crowded to suffocation. Judge Magrath presided. When the speaker declared, "This Union is dissolved," the enthusiasm of the people was beyond bounds; they rose to their feet, threw up their hats, and cheered till hoarse; outside, "Minute-men" from Columbia were parading, houses were illuminated, fireworks set off; the people joining in every imaginable demonstration of joy on this occasion, and cheer after cheer rent the air.

Governor Brown, of Georgia, made a strong resistance speech at Milledgeville, declaring the right of secession, and said if the federal troops attempted coercion, for every Georgian who fell in the conflict the heads of two federal soldiers should atone for the outrage on State sovereignty.

A correspondent, writing from Richmond, Va., says, " The secession movement is going forward with a rush. All the conciliatory letters that 'Old Abe' could write for a month would be of no avail in staying the progress of this movement. The South would not regard as sincere one word he might say in conflict with his matured and long-standing convictions. The crisis is come, and secession is inevitable."

November 13. South Carolina legislature adjourned, sine die.

November 14. Immense torch-light procession in Columbia, in honor of the action of the South Carolina legislature.

Florida, by her Governor, telegraphed to the Governor of South Carolina that she would stand by the gallant Palmetto flag.

November 15. Senator Toombs made a powerful secession speech at Milledgeville, Georgia.

Governor Letcher, of Virginia, called an extra session of the legislature, to assemble Jan. 7, to take into consideration the condition of public affairs.

November 17. Grand gathering of citizens of Charleston, S. C., to inaugurate the revolution. A mammoth pole was erected near the Charleston Hotel, and the hoisting of the State flag on it was duly celebrated. The pole was made of Carolina pine, one hundred feet high, and surmounted by the cap of liberty. Cables were stretched across the streets to prevent the passage of vehicles. A dense crowd was collected on Meeting Street, extending over two squares. The neighboring house-tops, windows and balconies were thronged with ladies waving their handkerchiefs. The flag was hoisted amid tremendous cheering and the wildest excitement; the Washington Artillery paraded, and fired one hundred guns as the flag went up; bells were rung, and the band played the Marsellaise Hymn. After the Marsellaise the band played the "Miserere," from "Il Trovatore," as a funeral dirge for the Union. At the same time the Charleston Hotel, the Mills House, and other large hotels, flung out the Palmetto flag, and the people *vowed* that the stars and stripes should never again wave in Charleston.

When the cheering, attendant upon hoisting the flag, subsided, prayer was offered by the Rev. C. P. Gadsden, invoking God as their refuge and strength, asking protection for the liberties with which their fathers were blessed, their commerce and their firesides, and praying to be inspired with courage, with a spirit of self-sacrifice, and a love of law and order. That God would consecrate with especial favor the banner of liberty which that day had been hung in the heavens, and graciously keep the city over which it floated, and finally make them that happy people whose God is the Lord.

7*

After the prayer, speeches were made, the speakers all addressing the crowd as citizens of the "Southern Republic." During the speaking, processions poured in from different sections of the city, with music and cannon, each saluting the Palmetto flag.

From the windows of dwellings were suspended banners with such mottoes as "Now or never;" "No step backward;" "The argument is ended;" "Stand to your arms;" "South Carolina goes it alone, — her trumps, Magrath, Colcock, and Conner, — with these she claims a march."

Secession badges worn by men, women, and children. M. L. Bonham, member of Congress from South Carolina, resigned his seat in that body. The prayer for the President of the United States was omitted in the Episcopal churches in Charleston.

Nov. 18. Georgia legislature appropriated one million dollars to arm and equip the State. Ordered an election of delegates to a State convention, to be held January 2, the convention to assemble January 9.

Nov. 19. Governor Moore, of Louisiana, ordered the legislature of that State to convene Dec. 10.

We learn from Richmond, Va., through reliable sources, that there was at this time (Nov. 19), fully armed and equipped, in Virginia, a force of one hundred thousand of the *elite* of the young men of the State, with a reserve force of one hundred thousand more; that they had purchased from the United States government, since October 1st, five thousand smooth-bore percussion muskets, which had arrived there, and that eight thousand stand of arms of different classes, purchased at the North, had been forwarded within the previous week.

Virginia entered into a contract for three thousand shells, to suit heavy artillery, besides five hundred barrels of Dupont powder, which had been purchased and stored at Lexington and Richmond. Two thousand new sabres had been provided for cavalry, besides one thousand old ones, which had been improved in a manner to suit any emergency; also one thousand revolving pistols of the Dean and Adams model, which were soon to be distributed. These were exclusive of the regular arms in the depot of the State.

November 20. Large arrivals in New York of arms for the South. Heavy orders received and filled in New York for rifles, ammunitions, pistols, etc., for the South.

Both branches of the North Carolina legislature convened. The Governor, in his message, recommended the enrolment of all men between eighteen and forty-five years, and also the raising of a corps of ten thousand volunteers, with arms and equipments. A correspondent writes: "Non-intercourse with the free States is decidedly the sentiment of the people, and domestic uniforms are becoming all the rage for the military companies.

A party of young gentlemen, of New Orleans, in whose chivalric hearts the secession fever raged intensely, resolved to wear no cloth but what was made south of Mason and Dixon's line, consequently ordered entire suits to be made for each one, of Kentucky jeans, and only discovered when too late that the goods were manufactured in Massachusetts.

November 22. The Washington and Philadelphia banks suspended specie payment. The banks of Baltimore and Richmond suspended two days previously. Notes of all Southern banks at a heavy discount in New York. The New York banks resolved to consolidate funds, and afford relief by a liberal line of discount.

Nov. 23. Suspension of North Carolina banks legalized by the legislature of that State. Numerous bank suspensions announced in Pittsburg, Pa., Trenton, N. J., and Charleston, S. C.

Great public meeting in New Orleans to organize a "Southern Rights Association," whose purpose is to aid in carrying the State out of the Union. A correspondent writing from New Orleans, says : —

" The Southern heart is fired at last to its fullest extent, and whether it has the ' constitutional' right to secede or not, it is now too late to argue, and no one will pretend to doubt its ' revolutionary' right to secede ; that a vast majority of the people of New Orleans are consolidated as ' minute-men' of the blue-cockade stamp ; that ' minute-men' are forming throughout the cotton States in legions, and that the tide of the ' impending crisis' has turned against the North, and you may soon look for such an ' irrepressible conflict' in the Northern States, when the hundreds and thousands of mechanics and laborers shall be turned out of employ, as the North has never dreamed of."

November 29. The Vermont legislature votes against a repeal of its personal liberty bill, — 125 to 58.

The Mississippi legislature authorized the Governor to appoint as many commissioners as he might deem necessary, to visit each of the slave-holding States, to inform them that the Mississippi legislature had authorized a convention to consider the necessary steps for meeting the crisis. The commissioners were to solicit the co-operation of legislatures to devise means " for their common defence and safety."

By dispatches from New Orleans we learn that the excitement in that city was immense, and the secession feeling momentarily increasing. Disunion was regarded as inevitable.

The bank bill to suspend specie payment of banks in Georgia re-passed over the Governor's veto.

A bill was introduced into the house of the Georgia legislature prohibiting the levying of any execution from the courts of the United States on the property of citizens of Georgia, prior to December, 1861, — all sales under such process to be void.

We copy the following from a "Connecticut paper." We do not vouch for the truth of the statement, but it is rather spicy, and we give it to our readers as we receive it.

"A young lady from Vermont, teaching in a town in Georgia, writes to her parents thus: —

"'The people here are very much excited over the election of Mr. Lincoln. Yesterday they formed a military company among the young men, with a view to the exigencies of the hour, and to-day they came out to drill. The most remarkable part of that performance, to a Yankee girl, was to see each soldier have a negro along to carry his gun.'"

By advices from Florida, we learn that secession flags were flying in many portions of the State, and that the secession feeling largely predominated.

The following is an extract from the message of Governor Perry to the legislature of Florida: —

"I most decidedly declare that, in my opinion, the only hope the Southern States have for their domestic peace and safety, or for future respectability and prosperity, is dependent on their action now, and that the proper action is secession from our faithless, perjured confederates."

CHAPTER V.

Our Union is river, lake, ocean, and sky;
Man breaks not the medal when God cuts the die;
Though darkened by sulphur, though cloven with steel,
The blue arch will brighten, the waters will heal.

ATLANTIC MONTHLY.

DECEMBER 1. A committee of citizens of Texas, composed of leading men, petitioned Governor Houston to convene the legislature. The Governor responded that the present agitation throughout the country, and particularly in the South, arising from the election of a President and Vice-President upon a sectional issue, called for the calm deliberation of statesmen. That the assembling of delegates from sovereign States, in a consultative character and within the scope of their constitutional powers, "to preserve the equal rights of such States in the Union," might result in the adoption of such measures as would restore harmony between the two sections of the Union; and should such a convention be called, he would, upon receipt of information as to the time and place of its assembling, immediately order an election of seven delegates to represent Texas in the same. That he could see no reason for involving the State in the expenses incident to a session of the legislature, and altogether viewing the measure unwise, he could not convene it; but, if a majority of the citizens of the State petitioned for it, he would not stand in the way, adding, "We have the Constitution to maintain, and in maintaining the Constitution we must maintain our rights; when the Constitution fails to give them to us, I am for revolution. My action has been prompt, decided and legal. Finding a course marked out for me by law, I have followed it, and am now awaiting a response."

The secession feeling largely predominated in the southern and eastern portion of the State.

Florida legislature passed the convention bill unanimously. The convention to meet January 3d.

Banks in Georgia generally suspended specie payment.

Immense secession meeting at Memphis, Tennessee. Resolutions were passed, calling upon the Governor to convene the legislature, directing that a State convention be called, and telling the Southern States that Tennessee would stand by the action of the Southern convention for weal or woe. To show the state of feeling at the South, we copy portions of an extract from a letter written by Brigadier General Semmes, a graduate of West Point, in acknowledgment of the high honor conferred upon him; having been appointed to the command of the military department of Columbus, Ga. He says:—

" Southerners have a high and sacred duty to perform, and know well how to perform that duty. 'He who dallies is a dastard; he who doubts is damned;' and he who cries peace, union, when there is no peace, no union, and never can be, with a fanatic and infidel people who repudiate God and the Bible, deserves everlasting execration. I rejoice at the dawning of the day which is to separate us, I trust forever, from such a people,—a people who, folding the arms of the federal government around the South, stand behind filching from their pockets,—a people who, through the operations of federal law, rob the South annually of one hundred and five millions of dollars. No wonder they love 'the Union,'—the 'glorious Union.' It enriches them, by robbing us. Eternal hostility, say I, to such people, and rebellion to their accursed federal misrule. Separated from them they are impotent to harm us. Their voices, their hands (in our pockets) we dread ; their bayonets, themselves, we despise. Let a united South rally and strike down this God-forsaken Union with robbers, fanatics, incendiaries, assassins, infidels. Southrons, arise ! Buckle on your armor; trust in God and strike for independence. His right arm will support you.

(Signed.)   Paul J. Semmes.

Rev. P. N. Lynch, Catholic Bishop of Charleston, declined to go to the South Carolina convention, and withdrew his name from the list of candidates. ·He said, " There is another sphere in which I can more appropriately, and perhaps with equal efficiency, serve our State. In that sphere I trust I shall not be found wanting in my devotion to her interests, in weal or woe."

December 3. Preamble and resolutions adopted in the Georgia legislature, proposing a conference of the Southern States at Atlanta, on the 20th of February, to counsel and advise as to the mode and manner of resistance to the North in the existing exigency. The preamble and resolutions took strong grounds in favor of having all sectional questions finally settled, and objected to separate action.

Congress met at Washington, — President Buchanan's message read to both Houses, and transmitted to the South. It was conservative in its general character, and created but little remark, except with some few leading politicians. It did not please the extremists on either side. The following fiery declaration of Governor Wise, of Virginia, will define *his position*, and show in what light he regarded the President's message.

A gentleman writing from Williamsburg, Va., Dec. 4, 1860, says: " Meeting Governor Wise to-day, I took occasion to ascertain his opinion upon the latest phase of the sectional difficulties. The Governor says he regards the President's message as the most damning production that ever came from the pen of any President; that he (Wise) is prepared to maintain, to the last extremity, the right of any State to secede; but, while maintaining the right, he disagrees with South Carolina as to the policy. He is in favor of revolution, — of fighting in the Union, and of maintaining the rights of the South in the Union. He can 'wake up' twenty thousand men who will fight to the death for their rights under the Constitution in the Union, easier than he can one thousand to fight the Union outside. He would seize upon the forts and arsenals within the State, and never give them up until guarantees from the North are obtained that shall be satisfactory to the Southern States; but he declared that if Virginia shall not now insist upon her rights, either in the Union or out of it, so help him God, from that day he will be an emancipationist. He will not consent longer to be the owner of slaves, and allow his rights, as such, under the Constitution, to be set at defiance. Whenever a convention shall be called he will again take the field to secure the election of delegates who will carry out his mode of action. He wants no national convention and no compromises. War to the knife is his policy, until justice shall be accorded."

The same correspondent gives as his opinion, from all he had been able to learn, though a singular fact, and illustrative of how much the politicians have had to do in getting up the disunion feeling which prevails in Virginia, that, as a general rule, the largest owners of slaves are the most conservative and strongest Union men. It is the men who have the least material interest in the security of slave property who are the disunionists of Virginia,— who are in favor of disrupting all the ties which bind us to the Union, without waiting for an overt act on the part of the President elect.

December 6. The legislature of South Carolina passed a bill to place the State upon a war footing. It authorized the government to call into service ten thousand

8

volunteers. During the discussion in the legislature, Mr. Rhett said there had been for several years in Charleston eight of the largest size Paixhan guns, which might, perhaps, be used in taking the forts.

Mr. Marshall said the State had 382 infantry companies, 50 cavalry, 18 artillery and 62 rifle companies,— making 121 battalions, 56 regiments, 14 brigades, and 5 divisions. Mr. McGowan said the total military force was 65,000.

December 7. A circular was issued inviting the members of the Texas legislature to assemble in Austin, on the third Monday in December, for the purpose of holding an extra session, and to take the necessary steps for calling a State convention. Governor Houston declared his intention to resign, if the people of the State demanded the convoking of the legislature. This step, together with the unremitting exertions of the Governor to smother the flame of disunion, which had sprung up in the breasts of the people of Texas, rendered him very unpopular. Lone star flags were hoisted in many of the towns in Texas; and the people throughout the State appeared to be united in their feeling of resistance to the administration of Mr. Lincoln. We are permitted to make an extract from a letter received by a gentleman in New York, from a friend in Texas, a planter. He says, " Upon this subject our minds are deliberately, fully and unalterably made up. We are for secession, disunion, civil war, pestilence, loss of property, of life, or anything you can imagine, rather than submit to the rule of Lincoln, elected as he was by a purely sectional vote, and pledged as he is to a course of policy so ruinous to the South. The 'Lone Star' is flying in every direction, and there seems to be a settled determination not to submit."

December 8. The Kentucky banks resolved to continue specie payment, as a suspension could afford no commercial relief.

December 9. Governor Brown, of Georgia, published a long letter, favoring immediate secession.

December 10. An extra session of the Louisiana legislature convened at Baton Rouge. The message of Governor Moore was read. It recommended the *immediate* action of Louisiana, before the inauguration of Lincoln; that a conference of slave States be held; it asserts the right of secession, and asks half a million of dollars to establish a military board, to buy and distribute arms.

December 11. The military bill passed both houses, appropriating half a million to arm the State for defence, and for establishing military depots. Also a bill providing for the election of delegates to the State convention, to be held at Baton Rouge, on the twenty-third of January, passed both houses.

Legislature adjourned on the 12th sine die.

December 12. The Sixteenth Regiment of South Carolina Militia mustered at Charleston, six hundred strong. Their strange appearance at that time provoked a good deal of comment.

A paragraph in the Charleston Mercury says " that the repeal of the Northern personal liberty bills will have no effect on South Carolina to keep her in the Union; that, so far as the cotton States are concerned, these laws, excepting the insult they convey to the South and the faithlessness they indicate in the North, are not of the slightest consequence.

December 15. From the Galveston (Texas) News, we learn that military preparations were going on rapidly in all parts of the State, companies of " minute-men " were forming in all the southern and eastern counties, organizing, arming, and drilling were progressing, and the wildest enthusiasm prevailed, so much so, that ministers of the gospel forgot their high calling, or their "*occupation was gone*," as we find on the list of recruiting officers the name of Rev. R. W. Peirce, and that a company of sixty-five minute-men was enrolled in the cause of "treason" in consequence of an enthusiastic address by the Rev. Mr. Wilson; also, on the 30th of November, says the "News," a regiment of mounted riflemen, two hundred strong, paraded under the command of the Rev. James C. Wilson. The parade was witnessed by a large assemblage, including a host of ladies. At eleven A. M., the "minute-men" formed on the Plaza, around the liberty-pole, from which the Lone Star flag floated. The regiment was organized by the election of field and staff officers; the Rev. James C. Wilson chosen Colonel. The warmest military feeling was manifested. While Henry Ward Beecher and others, under the garb of Christianity, advocate disunion, and excite men to discord and strife on the "field of argument," these Rev. gentlemen band together to carry out treason's plot on the "field of battle."

December 17. The South Carolina convention met at Columbia, in the new and commodious church of the Baptist congregation. The galleries and seats on the floor reserved for spectators were densely crowded. The church was fitted up with every convenience for dispatching the business of the convention.

A banner was suspended over the pulpit, presenting to the audience the inscription, " South Carolina Convention of 1860 ; " on its reverse were inscribed the following passages from the sacred Scriptures : " God is our refuge and strength — a very present help in trouble; therefore will we not fear, though the earth be removed, though the mountains be carried into the sea. The Lord of Hosts is with us, the God of Jacob is our refuge." Francis W. Pickens was inaugurated Governor of South Carolina, before the legislature, the convention, and an immense concourse of citizens. The convention was organized and General Jamison elected President, when a motion was made to adjourn to Charleston, owing to the prevalence of small-pox at Columbia.

Mr. Miles spoke earnestly, and at some length, against removal to any other point, until the ordinance of secession was passed ; he says, " I think every question is subsidiary to this great and important matter of withdrawing the State of South Carolina from the Union; such a step, should we previously adjourn, would disconcert our friends and gladden our enemies. We would be sneered at. It would be asked on all sides, Is this the chivalry of South Carolina? They are prepared to face the world, but they run away from the small-pox. I am just from Washington, where I have been in continual conference with our friends. The last thing urged on me by our friends from the slave States was, take South Carolina out of the Union the instant you can. Now, Sir, when the news reaches Washington that we met here, that a panic arose about a few cases of small-pox in the city, and that we forthwith scampered off to Charleston, the effect would be ludicrous."

Mr. Carroll recommended that the delegates be vaccinated. If every member of the convention would resort to vaccination, there would be no danger, and in ten days time nothing would be heard of the small-pox. Yet, notwithstanding these arguments, the motion was carried, and they adjourned to Charleston.*

The members of the convention and of the legislature on their arrival in Charleston were received with great rejoicing. A salute of fifteen guns was fired, for the fifteen slave States, by the Marion Artillery. A battalion of the State Cadets were also present. Major Stevens, commanding the Cadets, addressed President Jamison of the

* We perfectly agree with Mr. Miles in thinking the "effect would be ludicrous," and *especially* with Mr. Carroll. The idea of a "*gallant band*" of one hundred and sixty-nine men, going to be *vaccinated*, headed by the aforesaid gentleman, it would be ludicrous indeed.

8*

convention, saying that he had brought the young Carolinians, as represented by the Cadets, to do honor to the
sovereignty of the State. General Jamison returned his
acknowledgments, and said " the convention comes prepared to sign the ordinance which shall make the State
free and independent."

The convention assembled at Institute Hall. There
were about one hundred and fifty delegates and about
seven hundred spectators.

The bill for arming the State of North Carolina passed
the Senate at Raleigh, by a vote of 41 to 3.

December 19. Committee appointed to draft a seces-
sion ordinance: Messrs. John A. Ingliss, R. Barnwell
Rhett, James Chesnut, Jr., James L. Orr, William Gregg,
Mr. Duncan, and William M. Hutson.

December 20. Mr. Ingliss reported the following ordinance : —

" We, the people of South Carolina, in convention assembled, do declare and ordain that the ordinance
adopted by us in convention on the 23d of May, 1788,
whereby the Constitution of the United States was ratified,
and all acts and parts of acts passed by the general assembly of this State, ratifying amendments to said Constitution, are hereby repealed ; and the union now existing
between South Carolina and other States, under the name
of the United States of America, is hereby dissolved."

The secession ordinance passed unanimously, one hundred and sixty-nine members being present, at 1¼ P. M.
The ordinance was ordered to be engrossed on parch-
ment, signed by the members; and placed in the archives
of the State at Institute Hall.

The news spread rapidly on the street, and a crowd
collected, and there was immense cheering.

The news of the secession of South Carolina created
intense excitement and rejoicing in Georgia and Alabama.

At a meeting of the city council of Augusta, Ga., in

" anticipation " of the passage of the secession ordinance by South Carolina, it was resolved by the city council of Augusta, that the person having in charge the bell commouly known as "*Big Steve*," be instructed to have said bell struck or rung one hundred times, as soon as the news is received that the State of South Carolina has resumed her sovereignty.

December 21. In Wilmington, N. C., one hundred guns were fired in honor of the secession of South Carolina.

At Portsmouth, Va., fifteen guns were fired for the fifteen slave States.

The " minute-men " of Norfolk, Va., met on the Stone Bridge, at one o'clock on the 21st, and fired a salute of fifteen guns in honor of South Carolina, and hoisted the " Palmetto flag." John Tyler, son of Ex-President Tyler, after the firing had ceased, mounted the gun and delivered a strong secession speech. Many ladies of the city congregated to witness the salute, and joined in by waving handkerchiefs. The following telegram was sent over the wires to the president of the Charleston convention : —

" The ' minute-men ' of Norfolk send greeting to South Carolina. With the glorious Palmetto flag thrown to the breeze, and floating over our heads, we have just fired fifteen guns in honor of the first step taken by that gallant State, and emblematic, we hope, of coming events. All honor and glory to the game-cock of the South.

" CHARLES HARRIS, *Chief of Minute-Men of Norfolk.*"

At Macon, Ga., the people were jubilant over the secession of South Carolina. There was a grand procession of " minute-men," parading, and bonfires, bells ringing, cannon firing, and streets illuminated ; all served to heighten the excitement and manifest the joy of the people.

At Montgomery one hundred guns were fired by order of Governor Moore, in honor of the secession of South Carolina.

At Pensacola the news was greeted with immense enthusiasm. One hundred guns were fired in honor of the event.

A dispatch from Mobile, Dec. 21, says: —

"The secession of South Carolina was celebrated here, by the firing, this afternoon, of a hundred guns, the cheers of the people, and a military parade. There is great rejoicing. The bells are ringing merrily, and the people are out in the streets by hundreds, testifying their joy at the triumph of secession. Many impromptu speeches are being made, and the greatest excitement everywhere exists."

There was an immense secession meeting at night, and "illuminations" in honor of South Carolina.

In New Orleans there was a general demonstration of joy consequent upon the secession of South Carolina. One hundred guns were fired, and the "Pelican flag" unfurled. Impromptu speeches were made by many of the leading citizens.

On the 21st, in Charleston, there was a grand procession of "minute-men," to celebrate the passage of the secession ordinance. Several thousand citizens, strangers, firemen, and military were in line, with music, banners, transparencies, and reflectors. The procession formed in front of Secession Hall, and proceeded to the Mills House, to serenade Governor Pickens, and subsequently to Wm. D. Porcher, President of the Senate, General Simmons, Speaker of the House, General Jamison, President of the Convention, and Mayor Macbeth, who acknowledged their thanks and compliments. The flag borne in front of the procession was that which Captain Berry, of the steamship Columbia, hoisted off Governor's Island. The city was alive with pleasurable excitement, and a number of residences, newspaper establishments, and other public buildings were illuminated.

The convention met at noon. Prayer was offered, in the course of which God was invoked to unite the people of the South in the formation of a "Southern Confederacy," and to *bless* the new-born State.

Lieutenants Dazier and Hamilton, also several midshipmen, Carolinians, resigned their commissions in the navy.

December 22. At Petersburg, Va., a secession pole, one hundred feet high, with the "Palmetto flag," was hoisted on the most prominent street, amid the cheers of a large crowd. The pole was sawed down the next morning before the dawn of day, by an unknown party, and the flag carried off. Great excitement prevailed in consequence.

December 24. Agreeably to the ordinance of secession, Governor Pickens issued an address, proclaiming to the world that South Carolina is and has a right to be a separate, sovereign, free, and independent State, and as such has a right to levy war, conclude peace, negotiate treaties, leagues, or covenants, and do all acts whatever that rightly appertain to a free and independent State.

An immense secession meeting was held at Ashland Hall, Norfolk, Va. Disunion speeches were delivered by Col. V. D. Grover and General John Tyler. The speakers were enthusiastically applauded. General Tyler concluded with the expression, "*Let the Union go to hell*," which was received with loud and repeated cheers.

The Methodist Conference of South Carolina passed resolutions favoring secession.

The special commissioners appointed by the South Carolina convention to negotiate for government property, and form a treaty of amity and commerce with the United States, leave Charleston for Washington.

An immense mass meeting was held in New Orleans, to ratify the nomination of the "Southern Rights" candidates for the convention. The Southern Marsellaise was sung, as the banner of the Southern Confederacy was raised, amid reiterated and prolonged cheers for South Carolina and Louisiana.

December 26. A resolution offered in the South Carolina convention, that the Governor be requested to communicate to the convention in "secret session," any information he possesses in reference to the condition of Forts Moultrie and Sumter, and Castle Pinckney,—the number of guns in each, the number of workmen and kind of labor employed, the number of soldiers in each, and what additions, if any, have been made since the 20th inst.; also, if any assurance has been given that the forts will not be reinforced, and if so, to what extent; also, what police or other regulations have been made, if any, in reference to the defences of the harbor of Charleston, the coast and State.

Major Anderson transferred the United States garrison at Fort Moultrie to Fort Sumter, leaving only a small guard in Fort Moultrie.

Only one short week had passed since the signing of the "secession ordinance," and the joyous excitement conseqent thereupon had scarcely begun to subside, when the city was startled with the intelligence of the evacuation of Fort Moultrie.

The wildest excitement seized the people, and in the fire of their indignation they denounced Major Anderson in the most bitter terms, and their rage knew no bounds at this, what they deemed, overt act on the part of the gallant commander. The military were ordered out, and the convention went into "secret session." Troops were tendered to the Governor from different portions of Carolina, Georgia, Alabama, and Mississippi.

December 28. The "Palmetto flag" was raised over the Custom House and Post-office at Charleston, S. C.

At five o'clock in the evening the "Palmetto flag"

was raised at Castle Pinckney, and a military force went over and took possession of Fort Moultrie.

Castle Pinckney and Fort Moultrie were held by about twelve men, who peaceably surrendered to the State troops.

The " Federal flag " was saluted with thirty-two guns as it descended, and the " Palmetto flag?" with one gun as it was run up.

A large and enthusiastic secession meeting was held at Richmond, Va.

One hundred guns were fired in Wilmington, N. C., on the twenty-eighth, over the secession of South Carolina, and we are informed that, in less than twenty minutes after the firing commenced, every vessel in port, with the exception of one, run up the "stars and stripes."

In a Troy, N. Y., paper we find a letter, dated December 28, from General Wool, stating that the " Waterveliet Arsenal " was exclusively under the jurisdiction of the Secretary of War, and that on the ninth of that month (December) ten thousand muskets were sold, by order of Secretary Floyd, to S. B. Lamar, of Savannah, Georgia, and were shipped from the arsenal on the fourteenth inst. The price was two dollars and a half for each musket.

An immense Union meeting was held at Memphis, Tenn. It was addressed by Hon. Neil S. Brown, and others.

Governor Hicks again refused to convene the legislature of Maryland.

In reply to a friendly letter from Capt. John Contee, of Prince George's County, urging him to call an extra session of the legislature, he says : —

" I have no party-attachments or prejudices that conflict with my love for the Union, or that can influence me in the endeavor to discharge my duty faithfully to my native State. I have long since decided to put aside party-feelings and prejudices, and do everything in my power to preserve and perpetuate the Union of the States and the happiness of millions depending upon it.

"We cannot shut our eyes to the fearful peril of the hour. We know that a dark cloud overshadows the land, threatening the destruction of the institutions we have been taught to revere, and under which we have grown to be a great nation. We know that reckless and designing men are endeavoring to precipitate a dissolution of the Union before the people shall have time for the reflection so imperatively demanded by the vast interests involved in the threatened separation, whether that separation shall be peaceful or bloody. There must be time to weigh well all the consequences before we proceed to destroy the government bequeathed to us by our fathers; and we should wait to see if there is not still enough wisdom, virtue, and patriotism in Congress and the country, to give the people time for the 'sober second thought.'

"It seems to me, from the hot haste with which some of the Southern States are pressing a dissolution, that their leading men appear to act deliberately, believing that the people would not sustain them in their reckless course if they had time to weigh the consequences, nor act without one more appeal to the people of the North. Does it not seem strange that we have only now realized the great wrong done the Southern States by the personal liberty bills enacted by the North? We know that these laws have been upon the statute-books of many of these States for years, and that until now they have never been considered a sufficient cause to justify the South in dissolving the Union."

After expressing the wish that these personal liberty laws might be repealed at once, and the rights of the South, guaranteed by the Constitution, respected and enforced, he closes by saying : —

"The time has indeed come when we must all look the

danger full in the face; when patriotism, the memories of the past, and the hopes of the future, imperatively demand that we should use every exertion compatible with honor to prevent the United States of America from disappearing from among the nations of the world.

"I shall be the last one to object to a withdrawal of our State from a confederacy that denies to us the enjoyment of our undoubted rights; but believing that neither her honor or her interests will suffer by a proper and just delay, I cannot assist in placing her in a position from which we may hereafter wish to recede. But I assure you that whenever, in my judgment, the necessity for assembling that body in ' extra session' shall arise, I shall not shrink from the responsibility.

"I have the honor to be your obedient servant,

"THOMAS W. HICKS."

CHAPTER VI.

Not a protest I heeded, nor Cass's note,
As my country to ruin I hurried;
Whilst *Floyd* discharged his farewell shot
O'er the grave where the Union I buried.
BUCHANAN.

DECEMBER 29. Secretary Floyd resigned.

December 30. Sunday. South Carolina troops took possession of the arsenal at Charleston; military preparations were actively progressing; volunteers were offering their services from other States, among whom were many army and navy officers. Colonel Walter Gwynn, a graduate of West Point, and an old United States army officer, accepted the command of a military company in Columbia, S. C.

Shipment of arms to the South.

The steamship Montgomery, which arrived at Savannah on the 26th of November, had on board 180 boxes of Sharp's patent carbines, 1,800 in all, and 40,000 conical ball cartridges, for the State of Georgia.

The Baton Rouge (La.) Gazette states that a telegram was received at the arsenal there, from the war department at Washington, on the 22d of December, ordering the sale of two thousand five hundred guns, for $2.50 each, to Governor Pettus, of Mississippi.

On the twenty-eighth of December we find there were sent, by order of Secretary Floyd, from the Alleghany Arsenal to Ship Island, near the Balize, mouth of Mississippi,—

21 ten-inch columbiads, 128 pounders.
21 eight-inch   "   64   "
4 iron guns,   32   "

To Newport, near Galveston Island, Texas,—
23 ten-inch columbiads, 128 pounders.
48 eight-inch   "   64   "
7 iron guns,   32   "
In all, one hundred and twenty-four guns, one broadside
of which would throw five tons of balls.

Floyd did a lively business in treason all around.

The superintendent of the Springfield, Mass., armory,
received an order from Secretary Floyd to deliver to
Major Thornton, of the army, having charge of the military stores in New York, twenty thousand muskets, as
condemned ordnance stores, and to be sold. They were
sold to the State of Virginia for two and a half dollars
each ; which cost the government twelve dollars each.

Twenty-six mounted field-pieces from the " Watervliet
Arsenal" were forwarded to South Carolina, January 3d.

During the year 1860, there was removed from the
Springfield (Mass.) armory, and deposited in other arsenals of the United States, 135,430 government arms, as
follows : —

Texas Arsenal	500
Charleston, S. C.	15,000
Mount Vernon, Ala.	15,000
Augusta, Ga.	20,000
Fayetteville, N. C.	25,000
Baton Rouge, La.	30,000
Benicia, Cal.	7,000
St. Louis, Mo.	2,530
New York, (sold South)	20,400
	135,430

Thus it will be seen that from the Springfield armory
alone there had been sent to the points where treason
had made its appointments, 128,000 muskets, and not a
single musket to any United States arsenal in a Northern
State, except 20,000 to New York. These, like those from

Troy, were not to remain in New York, but were sold to the traitors for the paltry sum of two dollars and a half each.

This removal of arms was entirely "independent" of the supply which the government sends, as the regular quota, to the different States, aside from this, that was going on as usual. Here we see the treason of Floyd developing itself. It was impossible for him longer to conceal his villany, and when the people demurred, he resorted to stratagem to quiet their fears, until he could accomplish his purpose. If anything was needed to rouse our people to the frightful treachery over which they had been sleeping, *this* should have been sufficient. When, if they started in their slumbers or began to rouse from their lethargy, and asked why was this vast movement of arms,. almost simultaneously, from so many different points, and at a time too when the cry of secession, civil war and bloodshed was wafted to us from the South on every returning breeze, they were answered, "It is *only* the ' regular quota ' which the general government appropriates yearly to the several States. The Southern States, not having as many volunteer companies and militia as Northern States, have not called for their share until now, and it has been credited to them year after year, which accounts for the large number which they receive at this time."

Some little excitement was. caused in New York by the heavy shipment .of arms South from the arsenal at Troy, and it was intimated that the arms were to be used for hostile purposes by the secessionists. They, the people, were told that the rumor in the latter respect was entirely without any truth; that no fears need be entertained of hostility; that the arms alluded to were manufactured at the United States arsenal at Troy, for the State militia of Georgia, in accordance with an order issued in May previous; that a similar order.for the State of South Carolina was fulfilled about the same time; that these " shipment " were not at all unusual, as during the past summer months one hundred and twenty-five thousand stands of arms were sent to the five cotton States, in accordance with the requisition of the Secretary of War.

When the people of Pittsburg, Pa., arose in their indignation and resolved to oppose by force the removal of the heavy guns from the " Alleghany Arsenal," they were quietly informed that " the manufacturer contracted to deliver them at certain points where requisition was made, and any opposition or restraint in their delivery by citizens would inure to the injury of the contractor only, should the service suffer by delay ; that the appropriation for the purchase of the cannon was long since made for the defensive works at those points, and the order for their removal thither was in accordance with law and regulation, without any reference whatever to political occurrences."

Thus, with these and all sorts of excuses, the people were lulled to rest, until the " war-note " sounded from the walls of " *Sumter* " which awoke them to the fearful reality. And if ever man is punished for the robbery of a nation's treasury, it should be that same John B. Floyd of Virginia, who leaves the earmarks of fraud throughout his whole administrative career.

January 1st. South Carolina convention passed an ordinance to define and punish treason ; that levying war against the State, aiding her enemies, etc., be punished by death. Oh, consistency, thou art a jewel! The convention was opened with prayer, by the Rev. Mr. Dupree. The following is a quotation from the appeal : —

"O God, wilt thou bring confusion and discomfiture upon our enemies, and wilt thou strengthen the hearts and nerves and arms of our sons to meet this great fire in the name of the God of Israel."

9*

Immediately fronting the president was a bust of John C. Calhoun in white marble, with this inscription on paper:

"Truth, Justice and Fraternity, you have written your name in the book of life; fill up the page with deliberation; that written, execute quickly. The storm is from the North. The day is far spent and the night is at hand. Our homes and honor summon the citizens to appear on the parade-ground for inspection."

A correspondent writes:

"The 'Palmetto Guards,' one hundred strong, are guarding the arsenal, under the 'Palmetto•Flag,' instead of the stars and stripes.'"

The flag adopted by South Carolina is a red ground, with a marine blue cross, on which are fifteen white stars, a large one in the centre, a white palmetto tree and crescent on the upper right-hand corner, next to the staff, the corner spaces all of red.

The chair, the table, the pens, and the inkstand used on the memorable night of signing the ordinance of secession, were ordered to be reverentially placed in the State at Columbia, and sacredly preserved for posterity to see.

January 2. Forts Pulaski and Jackson, and the United States arsenal at Savannah, were seized by Georgia State troops.

Fort Macon and the United States arsenal at Fayetteville were seized by North Carolina State troops, by order of Governor Ellis.

Military operations in Charleston were very active, and every point of importance was fully manned.

A censorship was exercised over the telegraph, and the city was nightly patrolled by the military.

It was proposed to starve out Major Anderson and his brave little band, and then attack them on rafts, with the aid of the batteries already erected.

The South Carolina commissioners, at Washington,

received a telegram from Governor Pickens, saying, "that he was notified of the departure of the revenue cutter Harriet Lane for Fort Sumter, with sealed· dispatches from Washington, but that she *could not* come over the bar *except* under the *white flag;* otherwise, she would be fired into by the South Carolina troops."

January 3. Florida State convention assembled at Tallahassee.

January 4. Fort Morgan and the United States arsenal at Mobile were seized by Alabama State troops. The arsenal contained six stand of arms, 1,500 barrels ' of powder, 300,000 rounds of musket cartridges, and other munitions of war. There was no defence.

January 5. South Carolina convention adjourned, subject to the call of the Governor.

Governor Pickens received a telegram from the mayor of New Orleans, pledging that city to support Charleston when the time for action arrived.

January 7. Alabama convention met at Montgomery.

The Governor of Virginia, in a message to the State legislature, condemned the hasty course of South Carolina, but opposed federal coercion.

The Mississippi convention met at Jackson.

Major Anderson's removal to Fort Sumter sustained by the United States House of Representatives.

January 8. Forts Johnson and Caswell, at Smithville, were seized by North Carolina.

At Washington, Jacob Thompson, Secretary of the Interior, called upon the President to know whether reinforcements had been sent to Major Anderson. The President at once informed him that the steamer "Star of the West" had been chartered, and was on her way to Charleston, with two hundred and fifty United States troops.

Later in the day, at a meeting of the cabinet, Secretary Thompson demanded of Secretary Holt to know if it was true that two hundred and fifty regulars had been dispatched from New York to reinforce Major Anderson.

Mr. Holt *refused* to answer the question, on the ground that Mr. Thompson had announced that he should resign when Mississippi decided to go out of the Union, and as she had, according to the latest reports, so decided, he was of the opinion that Mr. Thompson was the last man in the world to be informed of the detail of operations of the War Department.

Secretary Thompson then telegraphed Judge Longstreet, at Charleston, that troops had been ordered to reinforce Major Anderson, and immediately resigned his seat in the cabinet.

Three days previous, Mr. Toucey, Secretary of the Navy (although previously urging the reinforcement of Major Anderson), now, in company with Secretary Thompson, called upon the President, and informed him that 'he had heard of the movement of troops in New York, and that he wished to know the facts. The imbecile President stated that if any such orders had been given, he would have them revoked. He accordingly authorized the Secretary of War to telegraph the commander of the " Star of the West " to land the troops at Norfolk, or Fort Monroe, and not to go to Charleston; but the vessel had departed before the dispatch reached there.

The most intense excitement prevailed among the senators and representatives from the gulf and cotton States. They regarded the reinforcement of Major Anderson as a declaration of war, and telegraphed the Charlestonians to *sink* the vessel, if *possible*, before she landed her cargo.

Lieut. Chapman and Master Mills, of the ship Brooklyn, resigned.

National salutes were fired in honor of the battle of

New Orleans and the bravery of Major Anderson, in nearly all the principal towns and cities of the Northern States.

January 9. The "Star of the West," bearing reinforcements for Major Anderson, was fired into in Charleston harbor. The ship *immediately* displayed the "stars and stripes." As soon as the flag was unfurled the fortifications fired a succession of heavy shots. The vessel continued on her course with increased speed, but finding it impossible to reach the fort without heavy loss, concluded to retire, and put about and went to sea, the batteries still firing upon her until their shot fell short. Only *two* out of seventeen shots took effect upon her.

Lieut. Hall was then dispatched by Major Anderson to Governor Pickens, to know whether the authorities of Charleston authorized the firing. Upon learning from Governor Pickens that the act was justified by him, and also that his (Anderson's) position in the harbor had *only* been "tolerated,"—that it was only by forbearance that the State had so long permitted him to remain there,—Major Anderson deemed it proper to refer the matter to his government; therefore signified to Governor Pickens his intention of deferring all further action in the case until he should receive instructions from Washington, and expressed the hope that no obstructions would be placed in the way, and that he, the Governor, would give every facility for the safe departure and return of Lieut. T. Talbot, as "bearer of dispatches" to the President of the United States; which was granted, and Lieut. Talbot left Charleston late the same evening for Washington.

The Mississippi State convention passed an ordinance of secession. Great illumination at night; guns were fired and fireworks let off in honor of the event.

January 10. South Carolina took possession of the steamship Marion, to be used in the service of the State, by the Governor's orders, but afterwards returned her to the owners, Carolina paying damages.

The Florida convention passed an ordinance of secession.

Fort McRae, at Pensacola, was seized by Florida.

January 11. Alabama State convention adopted an ordinance of secession, 61 to 39. After the adoption of the ordinance of secession by Alabama, the doors of the hall were opened to visitors, and a splendid flag, presented by the ladies of Alabama, was conveyed to the president's stand, and formally presented to the convention. It was immediately raised over the Capitol, amidst the ringing of bells, the firing of cannon, and the cheering of the people. The most intense enthusiasm prevailed.

Judge Jones, of the United States District Court, for the Southern District of Alabama, declared the court "adjourned forever."

The United States arsenal at Baton Rouge, and Forts Pike, St. Phillip and Jackson, were seized by Louisiana State troops, without resistance.

Major Haskins, with two companies, refused to surrender the Baton Rouge arsenal; but, being surrounded by six hundred men, he surrendered, as the "better part of valor." The excitement at New Orleans was very great.

Grand banquet given to John B. Floyd, at Richmond, Va., at which the following sentiment was given : — "The Hon. John B. Floyd, the *worthy* son of a 'noble sire.' All honor to the Virginian who *spurns* the trappings of a federal place, *respects* a mother's rights, and *resents* a mother's wrongs." (Music, and three cheers for Floyd.)

January 12th. Fort San Carlos de Barrancas and the navy yard at Pensacola were seized by Florida troops.

Lieut. Slemmer, in command of Fort Pickens, refused to surrender that fort. The following letter to the Florida commissioner is brief and to the point : —

"FORT PICKENS, PENSACOLA HARBOR, January 16, 1861.

" Col. William H. Chase, Commissioner for the State of Florida : —

" SIR, — Under the orders we now have from the War Department, we have decided, after consultation with the government officers in the harbor, that it is our duty to hold our position until such force is brought against us as to render it impossible to defend it ; or until the political condition of the country is such as to induce us to surrender the public property in our keeping to such authorities as may be delegated legally to receive it. We deprecate, as much as you or any individual can, the present condition of affairs, or the shedding of the blood of our brethren. In regard to this matter, however, we must consider *you* the aggressors, and, if blood should be shed, that you are responsible therefor.

" Signed, by order of A. J. SLEMMER, First Lieut. First Artillery, commanding,

" J. H. GILMAN, Second Lieut. Artillery,
Acting Post Adjutant of Post."

January 16th. Colonel Hayne, in the name of Governor Pickens, demanded the surrender of Fort Sumter.

The people of South Carolina demanded of Major Anderson the immediate surrender of Fort Sumter, and notified him that they intended to *take* it, " cost what it would." Major Anderson informed them that he had no authority to act otherwise than to defend himself. He was willing, however, to refer the subject to the government, and that the President could take such action as he deemed proper.

Accordingly, Colonel Hayne was dispatched to Washington, and *demanded* of the President the *immediate removal* of Major Anderson and his forces from Fort Sumter, as the only means of preventing war and its long train of calamities. He informed the President that South Caro-

lina "was determined to take it at all hazards," and that,
to avoid bloodshed, he had been authorized to negotiate
for its purchase, and also of other public property in
South Carolina; but if the President *refused* to enter into
negotiation, and declined to give it up to the State, then
they are "determined to take it," let what will come;
that the "stars and stripes" that wave over Sumter *must
come down,*— if not peaceably, then forcibly.

The President refused to receive him in any official
capacity.

January 17th. South Carolina voted to organize the
nucleus of a standing army.

January 18th. Virginia legislature appropriated one
million dollars for the defence of the State.

January 19th. State convention of Georgia adopted
an ordinance of secession, 208 to 89. Alexander H.
Stephens and Herschel V. Johnson voted in the negative.
Tennessee legislature called a State convention.

January 23d. Mr. Etheridge, of Tennessee, in a speech
in Congress, declared secession to be "rebellion," and
should be put down at any cost.

January 24th. The United States arsenal at Augusta,
Georgia, was surrendered to Governor Brown.

January 26th. The Louisiana State convention adopted an ordinance of secession, 113 to 17.

January 28th. Texas State convention met at Austin.

January 30th. Revenue cutters Cass, Captain J. J.
Morrison, and McClelland, Captain Breshwood, surrendered to the Louisiana authorities by their commanders.

The United States Branch Mint and Custom House at
New Orleans were seized by the State authorities.

February 1st. The Texas convention passed a secession ordinance, subject to ratification by the people.

February 4th. The rebel delegates met at Montgomery, Alabama, to organize a confederate government.
Howell Cobb was chosen chairman.

February 8th.   Col. Hayne, commissioner from South Carolina, unable to get recognition, finally left Washington.

Governor Brown, of Georgia, seized New York ships in the harbor of Savannah, in retaliation for the seizure of arms in New York.   The ships were released on the tenth.

The Montgomery convention agreed to a constitution and provisional government, and on the 9th elected Jefferson Davis President, and Alexander H. Stephens Vice-President, of the " Southern Confederacy."   Little Rock arsenal surrendered to Arkansas.

February 18th.   Jefferson Davis was inaugurated President of the Confederate States of America.

February 19th.   Fort Kearney, Kansas, taken by secessionists, but was soon after retaken by Unionists.

February 21st.   Jefferson Davis appointed his cabinet: — Robert Toombs, of Georgia, Secretary of State ; Charles G. Memminger, of South Carolina, Secretary of the Treasury, and L. P. Walker, Secretary of War.

Governor Brown, of Georgia, made another seizure of vessels belonging to New York.

February 22d.   President Lincoln made the journey from Harrisburg to Washington in the night, in order to prevent an anticipated outrage in Baltimore.

The *ungovernable* rashness of the rebels was, at this time, *particularly* manifested in an attempt to assassinate the President on his way to Washington.   The friends of Mr. Lincoln, having heard that a conspiracy existed to assassinate him, set on foot an investigation of the matter, and for this purpose employed a detective of great experience, who was engaged at Baltimore in the business some three weeks prior to Mr. Lincoln's expected arrival there, employing both men and women to assist him. Soon after coming to Baltimore the detective discovered a combination of men, banded together under a solemn

oath to assassinate the President elect. The leader of
the conspirators was an Italian refugee, a barber, well
known in Baltimore, who assumed the name of Orsini, as
indicative of the part he was to perform. The assistants
employed by the detective, who, like himself, were strangers in Baltimore city, by assuming to be secessionists
from Louisiana and other seceding States, gained the confidence of some of the conspirators, and were entrusted
with their plans. It was arranged, in case Mr. Lincoln
should pass safely over the railroad to Baltimore, that the
conspirators should mingle with the crowd which might
surround his carriage, and by pretending to be his friends
be enabled to approach his person, when, upon a signal
from their leader, some of them would shoot at Mr. Lincoln with their pistols, and others would throw into his
carriage hand-grenades filled with detonating powder,
similar to those used in the attempted assassination of the
Emperor Louis Napoleon. It was intended that, in the
confusion which should result from this attack, the assailants should escape to a vessel which was waiting in the
harbor to receive them, and be carried to Mobile, in the
seceding State of Alabama.

Upon Mr. Lincoln's arrival in Philadelphia, on Thursday, the 21st day of February, the detective visited Philadelphia, and submitted to certain friends of the President
elect the information he had collected relative to the conspiracy. An interview was immediately arranged between
Mr. Lincoln and the detective. The interview took place
in Mr. Lincoln's room in the Continental Hotel, where he
was staying during his visit in Philadelphia. Mr. Lincoln, having heard the officer's statement, informed him
that he had promised to raise the " American flag " on
Independence Hall the next morning, the morning of the
anniversary of Washington's birthday, and that he had
accepted the invitation of the Pennsylvania legislature to
be publicly received by that body in the afternoon of the

same day. "Both of these engagements," said he, with emphasis, "*I will keep*, if it costs me my life. If, however, after I have concluded these engagements, you can take me in safety to Washington, I will place myself at your disposal, and authorize you to make such arrangements as you may deem proper for that purpose." On the next day, in the morning, Mr. Lincoln performed the ceremony of raising the flag on Independence Hall, in Philadelphia, according to his promise, and arrived at Harrisburg on the afternoon of the same day, where he was *formally* welcomed by the Pennsylvania legislature. After the reception he retired to his hotel, the Jones House, and withdrew with a few confidential friends to a private apartment. Here he remained until nearly six o'clock in the evening, when, in company with Colonel Lamon, he quietly entered a carriage, without observation, and was driven to the Pennsylvania Railroad, where a special train for Philadelphia was waiting for him. Simultaneously with his departure from Harrisburg, the telegraph wires were cut, so that his departure, should it become known, could not be communicated to any place on the route. The special train arrived in Philadelphia at a quarter before eleven o'clock at night. Here he was met by the "detective," who had a carriage in readiness, into which the party entered and were driven to the depot of the Philadelphia, Wilmington and Baltimore Railroad. They did not reach the depot until a quarter past eleven; but, fortunately for them, the regular train, the hour of which for starting was eleven, had been delayed. The party then took berths in the sleeping-car, and, without change of cars, passed directly through to Washington, where they arrived at the usual hour, half-past six, on the morning of Saturday, the 23d. Mr. Lincoln wore no disguise whatever, but journeyed in an ordinary travelling suit. It is proper to state here, that, prior to Mr. Lincoln's arrival in Philadelphia, General Scott and Mr. Seward, in Washington, had been apprised from independent sources that imminent danger threatened Mr. Lincoln in case he should *publicly* pass through Baltimore, and accordingly a special messenger, Mr. Frederick W. Seward, a son of Senator Seward, was dispatched to Philadelphia to urge Mr. Lincoln to come direct to Washington in a quiet manner. The messenger arrived in Philadelphia late on Thursday night, and had an interview with the President elect immediately after his interview with the " detective." He was informed that Mr. Lincoln would arrive by the early train on Saturday morning; and, in accordance with this information, Mr. Washburne, member of Congress from Illinois, awaited the President elect, at the depot in Washington, whence he was taken in a carriage to his quarters at Willard's Hotel, where Senator Seward stood ready to receive him. The detective travelled with Mr. Lincoln under the name of E. J. Allen, which was registered with the name of the President elect on the book at Willard's Hotel. Being a well-known individual, he was speedily recognized, and suspicion naturally arose that he had been " instrumental " in exposing the plot which caused Mr. Lincoln's hurried journey, and thereby defeating the traitors in their murderous designs. It was deemed prudent that he should leave Washington, two days after his arrival, though he had intended to remain and witness the ceremonies of the inauguration. The friends of Mr. Lincoln did not question the loyalty and hospitality of the people of Maryland, but they were aware that a few disaffected citizens, who sympathized warmly with the secessionists, were determined to frustrate, at all hazards, the inauguration of the President elect, even at the cost of his life. The characters and pursuits of the conspirators were various; some of them were impelled by fanatical zeal which they termed " patriotism," and they justified their acts by the example of Brutus in ridding his country of a tyrant. One of them was accustomed to recite passages put into the mouth of the character of Brutus, in Shakspeare's play of Julius Cæsar. Others were stimulated by the offer of *pecuniary reward.* These, it was observed, staid away from their usual places of work for several weeks prior to the intended assault, although their circumstances had previously rendered them dependent on their daily labor for support; they were, during this time, abundantly supplied with money, which they squandered in bar-rooms and disreputable places. After the discovery of the plot, a strong watch was kept, by the agents of detection, over the movements of the conspirators, and efficient measures were adopted to guard against any attack which they might meditate upon the President elect, until after he was installed in office.

Mr. Lincoln's family left Harrisburg for Washington, by way of Baltimore, in the special train intended for him, and as, before starting, a message announcing Mr. Lincoln's arrival at Washington had been telegraphed to Baltimore, over the lines that had been repaired that morning, the passage of Mrs. Lincoln and friends through Baltimore was safely effected. During the ceremony of " raising the flag on Independence Hall," on Friday morning, Mr. Lincoln remarked that he would assert his principles on his inauguration, though he were to be assassinated on the spot; — evidently referring to the communication made to him on the night previous. The number originally banded together for the assassination of Mr. Lincoln, as far as could be ascertained, was twenty ; but the number of those who were fully acquainted with the details of the plot became daily smaller as the time for executing it drew near. Some of the women employed by the detective went to serve as waiters, seamstresses, &c., in the families of the conspirators, and a record was regularly kept of what was said and done to further their enterprise. A record was also kept, by the

10*

detective, of their deliberations in secret conclave. Thus our country was saved from a great crime, and Maryland from a foul blot that would have stained her fair name, by precautions which anticipated and thwarted the designs of the conspirators.

CHAPTER VII.

Many and long were the prayers that were made,
And millions were bowed with sorrow,
Whilst they wept for the glorious land thus betrayed,
And bitterly thought of the morrow.

FEBRUARY 23. The United States property and army posts in Texas, with the exception of Fort Brown, which Capt. Hill refused to surrender under Twiggs' order, were delivered to the State by General Twiggs.

A private letter from a gentleman in Texas gives a brief account of the treason of General Twiggs. The following is an extract : —

" Before I was out of bed, with a great shout, heard half a mile, the arsenal property was invested, and every house was filled with men, next to the commissary and pay department. This was protected by two companies of regulars. All day the most intense excitement prevailed, the commissioners on behalf of Texas and Gen. Twiggs negotiating. Over one thousand men were under arms, all our bridges guarded, and every moment a conflict was expected. Finally, Twiggs ended in ignominy an infamous career, by giving up all; and by four o'clock the poor soldiers left their quarters and took to camp a mile out of town, and their places were filled by the *"Knights of the Golden Circle.* Only two weeks previous, Gen. Twiggs furnished these very K. G. C.'s with arms, who now drive him from his position."

Evidence sufficient has been received to show that Gen. Twiggs, in addition to being a traitor, most basely deceived all the officers under him. Had he resisted the demands of Texas, his whole force there would have stood by him to the last.

The demoralizing effect of secession has had no illustration more *ignominious* and more *shameless* than has been afforded by the conduct of General Twiggs. He has not merely violated his oaths and gone over to the insurgents, but has disbanded his army, and delivered up to the State of Texas the posts and property of the United States, — a scandalous betrayal of trust. On the lowest view which can be taken of military honor, his conduct was *infamous*.

Treason, such as characterized the career of Cobb, Thompson, Floyd, and Twiggs, would put to *blush* the traitor " Arnold," while such names as Lieut. Hamilton, Commodore Armstrong, Capt. Breshwood, and other traitor officers of the revenue service, should have been stricken in disgrace from the national muster-rolls, instead of receiving from Secretary Toucey the " Well done, good and faithful servants," and their names still kept on the rolls of the American navy, side by side with those who have either died in defence of their flag, or resigned from honorable motives.

March 1.   General Twiggs was expelled from the United States army.

March 2.   Revenue Cutter Dodge surrendered to the rebels at Galveston.

March 4.   Texas State convention declared that State out of the Union.

Inauguration of President Lincoln. Troops in Washington were under arms to prevent an apprehended attack from the secessionists.

The President's inaugural address appealed alike to the judgment and sympathies of the people. It enforced on the attention of all the value of the Union to' the individual as well as the country, to the humble citizen as emphatically as to the President of the United States; yet it did not seem to meet the approbation of the extremists of either party. . The rabid abolitionists of the North thought it too conciliating, while the fire-eating politicians of the South denounced it as being a declaration of war, and became exasperated that President Lincoln should express his determination to hold the government property and collect the revenues, though at the same time the city of Charleston, S. C., was in a state of rebellion, and ten thousand men under arms in the city and vicinity ; and . the tone of public feeling is well illustrated by the comments of the Charleston Mercury and Courier upon the inaugural address. The Mercury says : —

" If ignorance could add anything to folly, or insolence to brutality, the President of the Northern States of America has, in this address, achieved it. A more lamentable display of feeble inability to grasp the circumstances of this momentous emergency could scarcely have been conceived. That President Lincoln will attempt to collect revenue off the bar is now beyond a question. What then ? Here lies the question in which alone this State is directly concerned. What course is then to be pursued by the Southern government ? There are but two open. The one, immediate attack upon Fort Sumter ; the *other, to besiege and starve out the fortress. To attack the fort will not remove the men-of-war from off our bar. What, then, will be gained ? It is a question. To reinforce Fort Sumter is now only to hasten the period of starvation, for no ship-of-war can enter our harbor and land supplies. Should she succeed in running to the fort, she will be under the constant fire of three or four batteries, within telling and destructive distance. She must be quickly destroyed. In the mean time, our ships, or ships laden with our goods for foreign ports, may continue their course as usual. Even should a blockade be declared, it can in no way interfere with the egress and ingress of neutral bottoms in their ordinary avocations of trade. A duty may, doubtless, for the present, be collected on such imports as arrive here directly from abroad. Of this, reckoning must be made in the calculation of costs, pro and con. A' few months must settle the whole question. And the taking of Fort Sumter immediately cannot, as far as we can perceive, hasten that period. We will be little further when we have finished than when we begun, — minus some valuable lives."

The Charleston Courier breaks forth in the following impetuous strain : —

" Let the argument proceed to the next logical and necessary step, — an appeal to arms. We are as well ready as any free people can ever be expected to be found in advance of the actual onset; and that argument once applied, will bring us new forces and resources. We are ready."

March 5. Jefferson Davis appointed General P. G. T. Beauregard to command the Confederate troops at Charleston, S. C.

March 6. Fort Brown, Texas, surrendered by special agreement.

March 9. The congress of the Southern Confederacy passed an act for the establishment and organization of an army.

March 12. The Confederate commissioners, Forsyth and Crawford, sent a communication to the Secretary of State, Mr. Seward.

March 15. Secretary Seward replied to the communication, declining official intercourse.

March 16. The Montgomery convention adjourned to May 13.

March 18. Supplies sent to Fort Pickens were intercepted by the rebels.

March 22. A meeting was held at Frankfort, Alabama, opposed to secession.

March 28. The vote of Louisiana on secession was published in the New Orleans papers, as follows : for secession, 20,448 ; against secession, 17,296.

March 30. Mississippi convention ratified the Confederate Constitution, 78 to 7.

April 3. A long and exciting cabinet meeting was held in Washington, to take into consideration the most judicious means of relieving Fort Sumter, enforcing the observance of the laws, and preparing for emergencies which might arise.

Great activity was manifested in the Navy Department.

South Carolina convention ratified the Confederate Constitution, 114 to 16. .

Rebel battery on Morris Island fired into a schooner. No one hurt.

April 4. Virginia convention refused to submit a secession ordinance to the people, 89 to 45.

April 7. General Beauregard notified Major Anderson that intercourse between the city of Charleston and Fort Sumter would no longer be permitted, and that he could receive no more supplies from the town. Steam transport Atlantic sailed from New York with troops and supplies.

April 8. Lieutenant Talbot arrived in Charleston, as messenger from the Federal Government, and left again for Washington on the tenth. He held a conference with Governor Pickens and Gen. Beauregard, the nature of which was to obtain permission for an unarmed store-ship to take provisions to the starving garrison at Fort Sumter. Permission was refused. Whereupon Lieut. Talbot notified the Governor of South Carolina, in the name of the Federal Government, that supplies *would* be sent to Major Anderson, " peaceably if possible, otherwise by force." Lieut. Talbot was not allowed to communicate with Major Anderson at Fort Sumter.

April 9.   Steamers Illinois and Baltic sailed from New York with sealed orders.

April 10.   The floating battery of the rebels at Charleston having been finished, was mounted with four thirty-two pounders, two forty-two's, and manned by sixty-four men, and anchored in a cove near Sullivan's Island, in a position commanding the barbette guns of Fort Sumter.

South Carolina convention adjourned, subject to the call of the president.   Before adjourning, it passed a resolution *approving* of the conduct of Gen. Twiggs in resigning his commission and turning over the public property in Texas to the State authorities.

A special dispatch from Charleston, under date April 10, says : —

" About seven thousand troops are now at the fortifications.   Troops are pouring in from the interior in great numbers.   One thousand men were sent to the fortifications to-day, and eighteen hundred more will go down to-morrow.   Everything is ready for a collision.   A battle is hourly expected, for Fort Sumter will be attacked without waiting for the ' *abolition fleet.*'   The beginning of the end is approaching."

April 11.   The Confederate commissioners left Washington for Montgomery, satisfied that no recognition of their government would take place under President Lincoln.   The commissioners alleged that the " Montgomery government was earnestly desirous for peace, and that in accordance with their instructions, as well as their own feelings, they left no means unexhausted to attain that much-desired end."   They charged the administration with gross perfidy, and expressed their firm conviction that war was inevitable, and that the responsibility would rest on the head of the Federal Government.

Intense commotion was produced in Washington by the promulgation of an order calling out the entire mili-

tia of the District.   It was soon ascertained, however,
that the movement arose from precaution, and from the
immediate necessity of means of defence, in consequence
of information being received of a contemplated movement for the seizure of the city by the secessionists.
Near midnight, orders were issued for the assembling of
the militia at their armories in the morning, and officers
were engaged during the forenoon summoning the men.
Some twenty companies were inspected at noon.   Washington bore a decidedly warlike appearance.   Troops
were marching and countermarching through the streets,
and drums and fifes were heard in every direction.   Several hundred men were mustered into service in the course
of the afternoon.   Four or five companies marched to
the War Department and took the army oath to serve the
United States faithfully against all enemies or opposers.
The obligation was for three months unless sooner discharged.   Thirty-two members of Schaffer's National
Rifles resigned, rather than remain in the ranks under
the "flag of the Union" in the present emergency.   They
were mostly, if not all, Southern men.   Nearly a thousand
men were enrolled in the regular service from the District
militia.   Those who refused to take the oath of allegiance
were marched back to the armories, disarmed, and their
names stricken from the roll.

While these preparations were being made in Washington for the defence of the national Capitol, and the calls
of the War Department were responded to by many " stout
hearts and strong arms," Major Anderson and his little
band of half-famished soldiers, in Fort Sumter, were
visited by Senator Chesnut, who was deputized, with Chis-
holm and Lee, to carry a message from General Beauregard, demanding the *immediate* and *unconditional* surrender of the fort.   Major Anderson replied that his
" sense of honor and his obligations to his government
would prevent his compliance " with the demand.

11

Perhaps it would be proper here to state, that one of the delusions which has served probably more than any other to encourage the secessionists, is the idea that the laborers and workmen of the North were all ready for *insurrection* from want of employment. They fancied the laboring classes of the North were on the point of starvation; that all the Southern States had to do was to commence the war and then stand still, and the Northern laborers would fight their battles for them. Alas, for their credulity, they will learn soon enough that Northern workmen are the truest friends and supporters of the Union, and that the laboring classes are the most loyal citizens, who would not allow this government to be trampled in the dust, in the day when the Constitution and the laws are to be enforced.

Gen. B. F. Butler, of Massachusetts, talking with a South Carolina commissioner, the latter is reported to have told him, that if Massachusetts should send ten thousand men to " preserve the Union" against Southern secession, she would have to fight twice that number of her own citizens at home who would oppose the policy. " By no means," Mr. Butler replied. " When we come from Massachusetts we will not leave a single traitor behind, unless he is *hanging on a tree.*"

The following dispatch was received from Charleston, under date of April 11: " A formal demand for the evacuation of Fort Sumter was made at two o'clock to-day. Major Anderson refused to surrender. His reply is to the effect that to do so would be inconsistent with the duty he owes to his government. Hundreds of persons have been waiting for hours on the wharves, and other points of observation, to see the beginning of the conflict, among them a great number of ladies. The house-tops are covered with people, watching with feverish interest for the first signal of attack. The excitement in the city is intense; every train brings throngs of citizens and

soldiers to town ; twenty-two car loads came from Columbia to-night, and advices have just been received that
Georgia has ready fifty thousand men armed and equipped
for service.

"A call has been made for three hundred mounted
volunteers as an extra patrol in the city to-night. Over
one thousand have responded. The Sixteenth Regiment
has also been ordered on duty ; the Citadel Cadets are
guarding the battery with heavy cannon. The movements
at Fort Sumter are plainly visible with a glass. Major
Anderson has been busy all day strengthening his position.

"Senators Wigfall, Chesnut, Ex-Governor Manning of
South Carolina, Hon. Wm. Porcher Miles, ex-member
of Congress, and Pryor of Virginia, are on the staff of.
Gen. Beauregard, doing duty to-night ; stirring times are
at hand ; the ball may open at any moment with great
slaughter ; thousands are waiting to see the attack commenced."

It is estimated that between six and seven thousand
men were stationed on Morris' and Sullivan's Islands and
points along the coast. Every man capable of bearing
arms was called out ; and all to fight *sixty men.*

Major Anderson fired a signal gun at ten o'clock in the
morning, probably hoping to get a response from the
"fleet" coming to his assistance.

April 12. Hostilities commenced. At half-past four
o'clock in the morning, Fort Moultrie began the bombardment of Fort Sumter, after which the batteries at
Mount Pleasant, Cumming's Point, and the floating battery, opened a brisk fire with shot and shell. Everybody
was in a ferment ; some of those fighting were stripped
to the waist.

Fort Sumter remained silent, no signs of life or anima-
tion for two hours and a half, while the shot and shell
flew thick and fast from seventeen mortars and thirty
large guns, mostly columbiads, until seven o'clock, the

bombardment still going on, Major Anderson opened from the two tiers of guns looking towards Fort Moultrie and Stevens' Battery, and the *first* gun that was fired by the " Federal troops " in the war of 1861 boomed forth towards Moultrie.

The war cry was sounded — hostilities commenced, ran along the wires of the telegraph, reverberated among the hills of New England, and *aroused* the sturdy sons of Maine. The great heart of the North " stood still," as if in its suspended vibrations it might hear, coming from the far distant parapets of Sumter, the notes of victory.

The firing continued uninterruptedly during the day, Major Anderson dividing his shots between Fort Moultrie, the Stevens and floating batteries, and Fort Johnson, with all the skill and determination of a great military chieftain, worthy of his position, until six o'clock in the evening, when he ceased firing, and was engaged during the night repairing damages, and preparing for an early attack upon the enemy. The firing, however, was kept up all night on Fort Sumter. A bomb was thrown into the fort every twenty minutes during the night, but Sumter's guns remained silent until the morning broke, when Major Anderson commenced to return the fire of the " Confederates," which was kept up with unintermitting vigor.

At nine o'clock in the morning a dense smoke poured out from Fort Sumter, and it was soon ascertained that the officers' quarters, sheds, and wood-work of the fort had taken fire from one of the enemy's shells. They have now to contend with an *internal* enemy. Fort Sumter is on fire. The Federal flag is placed at half-mast, signalizing distress, while the shells from Fort Moultrie and the batteries on Morris Island fall thick and fast into Major Anderson's stronghold. The little garrison of Sumter are only occupied trying to put out the fire, — no time to return the shot of the enemy. The .

flames had forced the destruction of nearly all the powder, — ninety _barrels had been rolled out to prevent explosion; the cartridges were gone, and none could be made; the entire wood-works of the fort are one vast sheet of flames; a raft is thrown out, loaded with men, who are passing up buckets of water to extinguish the fire, — they now become objects of fire from Morris Island, and the balls are seen skipping over the water and striking the unprotected raft. Meantime Major Anderson's guns were silent. He allowed his men to be exposed to the galling fire upon them but for a few moments, then ordered them in and shut the batteries, as the smoke was too thick to work them. Fort Sumter is greatly disabled; several of her large guns are dismounted, two of its portholes are knocked into one, and the wall from the top is crumbling, and yet the " *stars and stripes* " still wave.

Shells from Cumming's Point and Fort Moultrie are bursting in and over Fort Sumter in quick succession. Every shot now seems to tell heavily. About one o'clock, P. M., the flag-staff was shot away, and the flag nailed to the piece and displayed from the ramparts. Three times Major Anderson's barracks were on fire, and twice he succeeded in putting out the flames, but the third time it was beyond control, and everything " burnable " about the fort was destroyed; the flames burst through the roofs of the houses within its walls, and dense clouds of smoke shot quickly upward. Major Anderson fired only *occasionally;* the guns on the ramparts of Sumter had no utterance in them; bursted shells and grape scattered like hail over the doomed fort, and drove the soldiers under cover; from the iron battery at Cumming's Point a continuous fire was kept up from three ten-inch columbiads, three sixty-four pounders, three mortars and one rifled cannon, while the floating battery and Fort Moultrie continued very regular and accurate, until half-past

11*

one, P. M., when Major Anderson, finding it impossible to hold out longer, or, at least, that resistance was vain, and despairing of any hope of help from the "fleet," run up the *white flag*, and an unconditional surrender was made.

After Major Anderson's flag-staff was shot away, Col. Wigfall, one of Gen. Beauregard's aids, went to Fort Sumter with a white flag, to offer assistance in extinguishing the flames. He approached the burning fortress from Morris Island, while the fire was raging on all sides, and effected a landing at Fort Sumter. He approached a porthole, and was met by Major Anderson. The latter said he had displayed a white flag, but the firing from the South Carolina batteries was kept up, nevertheless. The *double-tongued traitor* from the " cotton-fields of Texas " replied that Major Anderson must haul down the American flag; that no parley would be granted, and that "surrender or fight" was the word. Major Anderson then took down the stars and stripes, and displayed only a flag of truce. All firing instantly ceased, with the exception of one gun fired by Senator Chesnut, and another member of the staff of Gen. Beauregard, which was fired by way of "*amusement*" from Mount Pleasant, which made a large hole in the parapet. Afterwards, two officers of Gen. Beauregard's staff, with ex-Senator Chesnut and ex-Governor Manning, came over in a boat and stipulated with Major Anderson that his surrender should be *unconditional* for the present, subject to the terms of General Beauregard, after which he and his men were allowed to remain in possession of the fort, while Messrs. Chesnut and Manning came over to the city, accompanied by a member of the Palmetto Guards, bearing the colors of his company. These were met by hundreds of citizens, and as they marched up the streets to the general's quarters, the crowd was swelled to thousands, shouts rent the air, and the wildest joy was manifested. Three fire-engines were sent down to the fort, for the purpose of extinguishing the flames; but the fire had, however, been previously extinguished by Anderson and his men.

The "fleet" laid idly by during thirty hours, silent witnesses of the contest, and either could not or would not come to his assistance; probably, however, not being ships of war, they were incapable of rendering any material aid against such a powerful enemy. During the engagement, it is said, the soldiers in Fort Sumter were *perfectly reckless* of their lives, and at every shot would jump upon the ramparts, observe the effect, and then jump down, cheering, and yet no one was killed in Sumter during the action, and but four or five wounded, and the rebels *say* none was killed on their side, though quite a number were struck by spent pieces of shell and knocked down, but none hurt seriously.

After the surrender of the fort, a boat, with an officer and ten men, was sent from one of the United States ships composing the fleet in the offing, to Gen. Simons, commander of the forces on Morris Island, with a request that a merchant ship, or one of the government vessels, be allowed to enter and take off the commander and garrison of Fort Sumter. Gen. Simons replied that if no hostilities were attempted during the night, and no effort being made to reinforce or retake Fort Sumter, he would give them an answer at nine o'clock on Sunday morning. The officer signified that this was satisfactory, and returned. On Sunday, the fourteenth, the last act in the "drama" of Fort Sumter was concluded Major Anderson and his command, taking with them their wounded, left the fort and sailed for New York. He *saluted* his flag, and the company then forming on the parade-ground, marched out on the wharf, with drum and fife playing "Yankee Doodle."

The Confederate flag was raised over Fort Sumter late in the afternoon on Sunday, and the fort was garrisoned

by the "Palmetto Guards," under command of Lieut.
Col. Ripley, who took command of Fort Moultrie after
the departure of Major Anderson. A correspondent of
one of the New York papers, writing from Charleston,
says: "One of the aids carried brandy to Major Anderson in a boat after the fire, and the latter said it was very
acceptable, as the men were completely exhausted by
their labors;" the correspondent adds, "I mention this to
show the kind and chivalrous relations existing between
the officers."

Perhaps their ideas are sufficiently extensive to induce
them to believe it was a manifestation of "chivalry" in
ex-Senator Chesnut and his colleague to fire a sixty-four
pounder into a fort with a white flag flying from its ramparts, just for "amusement," or in firing upon an unprotected raft, covered with defenceless men, who, thoughtless of their own safety, are laboring assiduously to subdue the raging flames.

The excitement in Charleston, during the contest, is
said to be immense. The housetops, the battery, the
wharves, the shipping, and in fact every available place,
was taken possession of by the multitude. The streets
were filled with men, women, and children, old and
young, black and white. Some went to the battery, some
to the wharves, and some to the steeples of the churches,
to view the solemn spectacle, and many a tearful eye
attested the anxious affection of the mother, wife, and
sister, for those engaged in the contest. But with the
display of a flag of truce, and the announcement that
Fort Sumter had unconditionally surrendered, the bells
rang out a merry peal, cannon were fired, and the people
engaged in every demonstration of joy.

Troops poured into the city by hundreds, and people
were constantly arriving on horseback, and by every
other conveyance. Within an area of fifty miles, where
the thunder of the artillery could be heard, the effect

was magnificently terrible. It was estimated that two thousand shots were fired, and that ten thousand men were under arms in the harbor and on the coast. Fort Moultrie was badly damaged. The officers' quarters and barracks were torn to pieces. The frame-houses on the island were riddled with shot in many instances, and whole sides of houses were torn out. The other fortifications sustained but little injury.

THE REBEL FORTIFICATIONS.

The nearest point of land to Fort Sumter is Cumming's Point — distance one thousand one hundred and fifty yards. On this point is a railroad iron battery. It consists of a heavy frame-work of yellow pine logs. The roof is of the same material, over which dovetailed bars of railroad iron of the T pattern are laid from top to bottom — all of which is riveted down in the most secure manner. On the front it presents an angle of about thirty degrees. There are three port-holes, which open and close with iron shutters of the heaviest description. When open, the muzzles of the columbiads fill up the space completely. The recoil of the gun enables the shutters to be closed instantly. The guns of the work bear on the south wall of Sumter, the line of fire being at an angle of about thirty-five degrees.

The Fort Johnson batteries consist of two huge sand works, containing mortar and siege-gun batteries.

These works are one and one-fourth of a mile from Fort Sumter, and at present manned by two companies of regular artillery.

The Fort Morris battery, on Morris Island, has three columbiads and four mortars, which can be used either for Fort Sumter or for the channel, being *en barbette*.

Green's battery has four columbiads and two forty-two pounders *en barbette*, which will sweep the whole island.

There are on this island twelve batteries in all. Besides these are Castle Pinckney, on the lower end of Shute's Folly Island, Fort Moultrie, on a peninsula opposite Fort Sumter, and several works lower down to guard the entrance of the port.

A rather amusing anecdote is told of an old slave, who passed through the hottest fire, with a sloop-load of wool, on Friday evening, and came safely to the city. Somebody told him he would be killed in the attempt. " Can't help dat," said he, " must go to de town to-night. If anybody hurt dis chile or dis boat, massa see him about it shuah." His sloop received four shots.

CHAPTER VIII.

Still, as in battle's fiery front,
I saw my country's flag unrolled,
Meet the dread storm's impetuous brunt,
And fling the tempest from its fold.

LUNT.

THE news of the attack on Fort Sumter created a profound sensation throughout the entire North. It would be impossible to give even a faint idea of the excited state of the public mind, — words are inadequate to express anything like the reality.

We pause to contemplate the terrible event, the commencement of actual warfare between two portions of the United States, — brother against brother. But the great fact is upon us. Civil war has been commenced, and there are few among us who are ready to see this glorious government prostrate in the dust at the feet of traitors. Fraternal blood must be shed, the government *must* be sustained.

Coincident with the surrender of Fort Sumter, the slumbering patriots of the free States awoke to the fearful reality that war was inaugurated. Party divisions and political factions were immediately sunk in one common grave; love for their country and loyalty to the government was the all-pervading spirit, — every countenance was wild with enthusiasm.

The " smell of battle " seemed to put new nerve into the sons of New England, and they arose in their might, and, with one heart, rallied around the standard for the defence of the " Constitution," irrespective of " party."

They came, as one man, ready to lay their lives on the "altar" of their country.

Telegraph and newspaper offices were crowded to repletion, eager for the least item of intelligence from the seat of war. The streets were literally black with human beings wandering up and down discussing the probable "attack upon the national capital," and the final result; while here and there an excited crowd, with tearful eyes, dwelt with generous ardor upon the picture of the long vigil in Sumter; the midnight transfer from Fort Moultrie ; and recounted the weary watch of the little garrison for reinforcements, which an imbecile and vacillating President ordered to-day and recalled to-morrow. They pictured the eighty men looking out daily upon the vast preparations made for their destruction; obedient to their orders to act only on the defensive; daily giving of their failing strength to add what little they might to the defences of their post; watching with anxious eyes their decreasing store of provisions, their brave hearts never faltering from duty. They spoke of the calm Sabbath morning (February 3) on which the women and children belonging to the garrison took their sad farewell of husbands and fathers, and sailed for New York, to find shelter from the coming storm. Over and over again did they describe the attack, made hastily, in fear of the arrival of reinforcements; the first guns, at early day, from Fort Moultrie; the reply from Sumter; the growing circle of fire around the devoted garrison; the crowds gathered in the city's front to witness the unequal strife, and rejoice in the attempt of six thousand men to slay eighty of their countrymen, — that in that solemn moment a late United States senator "fired a gun by way of amusement;" and that five thousand South Carolinian women, denying the gentle instincts of womanhood, gathered to view the bloody spectacle, ready to respond to any sacrifice that might be required of them; not forgetting to relate, with wondering scorn, that even in this great crisis of the nation's history there was here and there to be found at the ‾ " North" a handful of *pitiful traitors* to glory in the progress of treason.

The 12th of April, 1861, is a day ever memorable in our annals, — treason has risen from blustering words to *cowardly* deeds. They have deliberately chosen the issue of battle; he who hesitates in his allegiance is a traitor with them. But there was no hesitation. The country responded as one man to the call upon its resources, and thousands on thousands of freemen only waited for the " war note " to be sounded from the national capital, to take up arms and march to the battle-field. The glorious old " stars and stripes " were simultaneously thrown to the breeze from millions of dwellings, stores, and public buildings, and suspended across the principal streets and avenues in the greatest profusion ; some large buildings displayed miniature " flags " from each and every window ; many public buildings, stores, etc., were decorated with festoons of red, white, and blue, bearing appropriate mottoes, surmounted by an eagle, shield, or some other emblem of liberty. Union rosettes and badges were universally adopted by men, women, and children. The greatest enthusiasm was manifested throughout the entire free States.

> When slumbering Treason woke at last
>   On South Carolina's soil,
> And all the patriots' hopes were past
>   To avert the fatal broil ; —
>
> When the first white smoke that curled above
>   The cannon on the beach,
> And the ball was sped at " Sumter's walls,"
>   To make the deadly breach ; —
>
> Then Northern heroes went to arms,
>   Looking to God above
> To care for wives and children left,
>   And shield them with his love.

12

"Give us," they cried, "from heaven above,
    The stars and azure blue,
And we will make the stripes *ourselves!*" —
    They've kept their promise true.

Our gallant sailors on the deep
    Have *twice* flung to the breeze
Our good old flag on hostile forts,
    Among palmetto trees.

And though we mourn for those who fell
    For the land they *died* to save,
Still we feel a glow of honest pride
    That they fill a " patriot's grave."

April 15th.   President's proclamation issued, calling for seventy-five thousand volunteers, and commanding the rebels to return to peace within twenty days ; also calling for an extra session of Congress, to convene July 4th.

BY THE PRESIDENT OF THE UNITED STATES — A PROCLAMATION.

Whereas, the laws of the United States have been for some time past and now are opposed, and the execution thereof obstructed, in the States of South Carolina, Georgia, Alabama, Florida, Mississippi, Louisiana and Texas, by a combination too powerful to be suppressed by the ordinary course of judicial proceedings, or by the powers vested in marshals by the law ; now, therefore, I, Abraham Lincoln, President of the United States, in virtue of the power in me vested by the Constitution and the laws, have thought fit to call forth, and hereby do call forth, the militia of the several States of the Union, to the aggregate number of seventy-five thousand, in order to suppress said combinations and to cause the laws to be duly executed.   The details of this object will be immediately communicated to the State authorities through the War Department.

I appeal to all loyal citizens to facilitate and aid this

effort to maintain the honor, the integrity, and the existence of our national Union, and the perpetuity of popular government, and to redress the wrongs already long enough endured. I deem it proper to say that the first service assigned to the forces hereby called forth will probably be to repossess the forts, places and property which have been seized from the Union, and in every event the utmost care will be observed, consistently with the objects aforesaid, to avoid any devastation, any destruction of or interference with property, or any disturbance of peaceful citizens in any part of the country. I hereby command the persons composing the combinations aforesaid to disperse and retire peaceably to their respective abodes within twenty days from this date.

Deeming that the present condition of public affairs presents an extraordinary occasion, I do hereby, in virtue of the power in me vested by the Constitution, convene both Houses of Congress. Senators and representatives are therefore summoned to assemble at their respective chambers at twelve o'clock, noon, on Thursday, the fourth day of July next, and there to consider and determine such measures as in their wisdom the public safety and interest may seem to demand.

In witness whereof I have hereunto set my hand and caused the seal of the United States to be affixed.

Done at the city of Washington, this fifteenth day of April, in the year of our Lord eighteen hundred and sixty-one, and of the independence of the United States the eighty-fifth.

(Signed)   ABRAHAM LINCOLN.

By the President,

WILLIAM H. SEWARD, Secretary of State.

The requisition from Washington for troops came to the Governor of Massachusetts by telegraph, at about two o'clock, on the fifteenth, calling for two regiments of ten

companies of sixty-four men each. It was requested that
the companies be got ready as soon as possible, and forwarded, by companies, immediately to Washington.

The Governor had a consultation with his staff, and
finally decided upon ordering out the Third, Fourth, Sixth
and Eighth Regiments of infantry. The following order
was accordingly issued: —

COMMONWEALTH OF MASSACHUSETTS.

HEAD QUARTERS, BOSTON, April 15, 1861.

Special Order No. 14.

You are hereby ordered to muster the regiment under
your command, in uniform, on Boston Common *forthwith*,
in compliance with a requisition made by the President
of the United States. The troops are to go to Washington. The regimental band will be dispensed with.

By order of his Excellency JOHN A. ANDREW, Governor
and Commander-in-Chief.

WILLIAM SCHOULER, Adj. General.

To Cols. Edward F. Jones, 6th Regiment; Abner B.
Packard, 4th Regiment; David W. Wardrop, 3d Regiment; Lt. Col. Timothy Munroe, 8th Regiment.

Major Cook, of the Boston Light Artillery, had tendered
the services of his company, but the Governor did not
feel at liberty to accept the offer, as the call of the President was for infantry only.

The Third Regiment was commanded by Col. David W.
Wardrop, of New Bedford, and consisted of six companies,
one from each of the towns of Halifax, Plymouth, Free-
town, Plympton and Carver, and the city of New Bedford.

The Fourth Regiment was commanded by Col. Abner
B. Packard, of Quincy, and consisted of companies from
Canton, Easton, Braintree, Randolph, Abington, Foxboro',
Taunton, Quincy and Hingham.

The Sixth Regiment was commanded by Col. Edward F. Jones, of Lowell. It consisted of four companies from Lowell, two from Lawrence, and one from Groton and Acton — making eight.

The Eighth Regiment was commanded by Lieut. Col. Timothy Munroe, of Lynn, Col. Coffin having recently resigned. It consisted of three companies from Marblehead, two from Lynn, and one each from Newburyport, Beverly and Gloucester.

Lieut. Col. Munroe raised five hundred volunteers in Lynn, on Monday evening, the 15th, in addition to the two companies belonging to his regiment. A purse of five hundred dollars was raised immediately to start with.

During the forenoon Gen. B. F. Butler tendered his brigade to the Governor, and several other officers of the Massachusetts Volunteer Militia made application to have their services accepted.

New York legislature voted thirty thousand men and three million dollars for putting down the rebellion.

Several Southern vessels, at New York, were seized and fined for irregular clearances.

Governor Magoffin, of Kentucky, in reply to Secretary Cameron's dispatch calling for troops, says,— " Kentucky will furnish no troops for the wicked purpose of subduing her sister Southern States."

Governor Letcher, of Virginia, in reply to the call for troops from that State, says, — " The militia of Virginia will not be furnished to the powers at Washington for any such use or purpose as they have in view."

Governor Ellis, of North Carolina, telegraphed to the President that he could not respond to the call for troops, as he had doubts of his authority and right to do so.

Governor Harris, of Tennessee, and Governor Jackson, of Missouri, also refused to furnish troops for the government at Washington.

Governor Harris says, — " Tennessee will not furnish a

12*

single man for coercion, but fifty thousand, if necessary, for the defence of our rights or those of our Southern brothers."

Governor Jackson says,—"The requisition is illegal, unconstitutional, revolutionary, inhuman and diabolical, and cannot be complied with."

The government of the Southern Confederacy called for thirty-two thousand men;—two thousand from Florida, and five thousand from each of the other seceded States.

April 16th, 17th, etc. General uprising in the North;—proclamations, military orders, voting men and money, the order of the day. In the principal cities mobs visited newspaper offices and firms suspected of disloyalty, and *compelled* them to raise the stars and stripes. Legislatures not in session were called together; banks offered loans to the government; great public meetings were held; and Union badges worn by everybody.

April 16th. The four regiments of Massachusetts volunteers, ordered to report for service in Boston, began to arrive there at nine o'clock in the morning; many of the men having left their homes with not more than two hours' notice,—dropped their tools, left their work-shops, their work half finished, bid a hasty farewell to wives and mothers, brushed away the falling tear,—and hurried off to respond to their country's call. That last hearty "God bless you!" which lingered upon the lips of loved ones, with many will remain the *parting words* until the morning of the resurrection.

Merchants, and business men generally, not only responded liberally to the demands upon them for money, but nobly and generously offered those in their employ, if any wished to go to fight for their country, that their salaries should be continued on, or duly paid over to friends as they should dictate, and the places kept for them until their return. Many patriotic hearts availed themselves of this opportunity, and left the counting-rooms and mercantile houses, and rushed on with the crowd to enrol their names among that mighty host to fight for the Constitution and the Union. The question soon arose, " What would become of the families of volunteers left without means to provide for themselves?" This question was no sooner asked than it was answered by generous donations from moneyed men and patriotic women, some contributing as high as two thousand dollars to the " volunteer fund," for the benefit of " soldiers' families."

On the morning of the 16th, the bark Manhattan, Capt. Davis, of and from Savannah, arrived at the port of Boston, and hauled in at Clapp's Wharf, No. 573 Commercial Street. As soon as Capt. Davis heard of the condition of affairs at the South he hoisted a secession flag, bearing upon it fifteen stars and a rattlesnake, at his main-mast head. It soon attracted attention from a number of people in the vicinity, and presently there was quite a gathering on the wharf. The crowd and the excitement continued to increase, and several men on the wharf demanded who hoisted the flag. The captain, who was walking up and down the deck, replied, — " I did, and mean it shall stay there." The cries and movements of the crowd became every moment more menacing, and the captain, fearing violence, retreated to the lower deck. Finally, the crew hauled the flag down, to save the ship from being damaged, and passed it to the crowd on the wharf. It was immediately seized, and torn into a hundred pieces.

The morning of the sixteenth of April was cold, dark and rainy, one of those gloomy mornings not much calculated to create enthusiasm among the volunteers. The order to assemble on the Common was countermanded, and the companies which first arrived proceeded directly to Faneuil Hall. Quite a crowd assembled on the Common at an early hour in the morning, and withstood the storm bravely for several hours, expecting every moment the troops would arrive, but to them no troops came. The depots were thronged, and when the trains arrived with the different companies and regiments, the greatest enthusiasm was manifested, and cheer on cheer rent the air.

The Marblehead companies, three in number, were the first to arrive at Faneuil Hall. They were received with hearty cheers by an immense crowd assembled in the street. When the order for troops was promulgated in Marblehead on the evening of the fifteenth, a subscription was at once started by the moneyed men of the place to provide for the families of the volunteers, who were mostly mechanics. In less than half an hour, one thousand dollars had been subscribed in sums of one hundred each, and next morning the amount was swelled to one thousand nine hundred.

The Marblehead companies were soon followed by the companies belonging to the Fourth Regiment. Faneuil Hall was filled by one o'clock, and the companies which arrived after that time were quartered in other places. The Third Regiment, Col. Wardrop, which came in on the Old Colony Railroad, occupied the hall over the depot, which was tendered to them by Mr. Holmes, the president of the road. The New Bedford City Guards, Capt. Ingraham, of this regiment, took dinner at the United States Hotel, and afterwards proceeded to the armory of the Second Battalion, which was tendered for their use. The Sixth Regiment, Col. Jones, came in on the Lowell Railroad, and first proceeded to Faneuil Hall, where they got dinner, and afterwards to the armory of the Second Battalion. The Eighth Regiment, Lieut. Col. Munroe, was divided, part being quartered at Fitchburg Hall and part at Faneuil Hall.

In narrating the praiseworthy promptness to respond to the calls of the country of our own American people, we must not forget our Irish citizens, for they were neither " last nor least " in this movement.

On the evening of the sixteenth, the Irish residents of Boston assembled in great numbers at the Jackson Club Room, Hanover Street, to express their affection for their adopted country, their firm determination to support the President of the United States in his trying position, and their abhorrence of the rebellious subjects who were engaged at the South in fomenting civil war.

B. S. Treanor, Esq., called the meeting to order.   On motion of Mr. James Sullivan, Captain Thomas Cass was appointed chairman for the evening.   The organization was further perfected by the choice of the following gentlemen for vice-presidents : —

Vice-Presidents — Dr. W. M. Walsh, T. H. Smith, B. S. Treanor, Owen Lappen, James Healy, Michael Gormley, John Maloney, J. H. Fallon, James Sullivan, Martin Lennon, John McGlinn, Wm. B. Maloney, Dr. John Walsh, Cornelius Murphy, W. W. Doherty, Michael Cummiskey, Jeremiah Lyons, John Kenney, Patrick McInerny, Dennis Hogan, Andrew D. Mahoney, James Dowling.

Secretaries — James Donnelly, Thomas A. Matthews, John Glancy.

The chairman then proceeded with his opening remarks. He thought the condition of the country was one fraught with momentous consequences to its adopted citizens. Our republic stands the last of all the great republics, and if this proves a failure, the experiment may never be tried again.   We have the blessings of home, liberty and equality, a free press, and religious tolerance to all. Nothing seems to be wanting to the happiness of the people, and their chief aim should be to preserve the government which ensures these blessings.   The success of the country has been an inspiration to the poor and downtrodden of all nations, not excepting unfortunate Ireland. We should resist every project and idea of disunion ; we

should resist all attempts to withdraw us from the love
of country, from whatever source they come. The young
men are now called upon to remember whose sons they
are, and from what blood they are descended. They
should bear in mind that death never comes too soon, if
necessary in the defence of one's country : —

> " Whether on the scaffold high,
>   Or in the battle's van,
>   The noblest place for man to die
>   Is where he dies for man."

B. S. Treanor, Esq., from the committee on resolutions,
next addressed the meeting in a speech which was received with great enthusiasm. He expressed the hope
that the adopted citizens might have an opportunity to
stand up with those who were native and to the manor
borne, upon the banks of the Potomac, in the defence of
the Federal capital at Washington. His allusions to the
Irish patriot Montgomery, and the soldier of foreign
parentage who led the American forces at New Orleans,
were received with general applause. Mr. Treanor at
this point read the following resolutions : —

" Whereas, for a long time previously, and ever since the
election of Abraham Lincoln to the office of the United
States, by a constitutional majority of the people, a dangerous and treasonable conspiracy has existed in several
of the Southern States, the open and avowed object of
which is the overthrow of the government and the destruction of the Constitution and the Union ; and,

" Whereas, this conspiracy was well known to members
of the late cabinet of James Buchanan, who had sworn
to maintain the Constitution of the United States ; yet,
regardless alike of their duty as citizens and officers of
the government, and in violation of their most solemn
oaths, they not only neglected to suppress this treasonable
conspiracy, but co-operated with the Southern traitors in

furtherance of their diabolical purposes, by plundering for their use the national treasury, and sending them government arms, intended originally for the defence of the country, to be used for its overthrow and destruction ; and,

" Whereas, in pursuance of this design, the traitors of the South have seized upon and usurped the dock-yards, arsenals, magazines, forts, custom-houses, public funds, and other national property in the rebellious States, and are now using them against the lives and liberties of the people to whom they belong ; and,

" Whereas, every peaceful effort made by President Lincoln to induce the rebels to return to their duty and their allegiance has met only contumely and insult from these misguided men, until the forbearance of the government was interpreted as evidence of its imbecility ; and at length ten thousand armed men have attacked Fort Sumter in the harbor of Charleston, and compelled the seventy brave defenders to surrender to their immense and superior numbers ; and that in pursuance of their treasonable designs the rebels now threaten to attack the seat of government and plant their despotic flag upon its Capitol,'—

" Be it therefore resolved by us, the adopted citizens of Boston, of Irish birth and parentage, in this the most dangerous and threatening crisis through which our beloved adopted country has yet passed, that it is the solemn and sacred duty of every citizen and of every man who participates in and enjoys the inestimable blessings and privileges of our free government, to cast aside all party distinctions and unite as one man in support of the national administration, and in defence of our common country, its flag and its freedom.

" Resolved, That we will support the government, by every means in our power, in its efforts to enforce the laws, collect the revenue, repossess the national property, maintain the Constitution, and suppress treason and rebellion wherever it appears.

" Resolved, that we call upon every adopted citizen of Irish birth to stand true to the country which has become the home of so many millions of our race and of the oppressed of the Old World, and not permit the liberties for which Washington fought and Montgomery died to be trampled under foot by the slave oligarchy of the South."

" What constitutional rights," continued Mr. Treanor, " of the Southern States have been in the slightest degree infringed upon ? Have we come to that state that the ballot-box shall be no longer the exponent of the people's will, or are we in that condition that the election of a new President must inevitably inaugurate a bloody civil war ? Secession interests have been cherished and nurtured at the South ever since Andrew Jackson squelched it in '33· The very rifled cannon that helped to batter down the walls of Sumter were sent to South Carolina by the traitors in the public service. Whatever soreness may have been felt by the adopted citizens at some of the past legislation of this State, they will be found ready, in the time of trial, to sacrifice every interest upon the altar of the country's cause, and as true to the national flag as those who rallied round it in the Revolution and the war of 1812.

" No supporters of a slave oligarchy would be encountered among the Irish race, who had experienced too keenly the discomforts of an arrogant government at home to desire a continuance of the same in the New World. The flag of the Confederate States shall never wave over Faneuil Hall, till every adopted citizen of Massachusetts bites the dust." (Great applause.)

Dr. Walsh made a speech to the same effect, and was followed by Dennis W. O'Brien, who apologized for a short speech on the score of indisposition, the subject being one in which he was deeply interested, and advised every man to do his best to support the Union, the Constitution and the laws.

Mr. T. M. Brown said the words they had heard should make music in the heart of every man born in the Emerald Isle. The place of every Irishman to-day is in the front. (A voice — "An' they niver was found in the rear!" Three rousing cheers were given for the author of this impromptu.)

The countrymen of Daniel O'Connell, of Davis, and others of the innumerable patriots of the land, are bound, by all that is holy, to stand by the glorious flag that has ever been true to them. The spirit which fought and won, and compelled a treaty on the old stone of Limerick, which nerved and fired the blood of O'Connell, — ay, the spirit of liberty is alive to-day, and the American flag shall never trail in the dust while Irishmen live to defend it.

Remarks were also made by James Sullivan, Edward Ray and others, and the resolutions were unanimously adopted. The meeting adjourned with cheers for the Union and the stars and stripes.

The banks of Boston offered to the State government a loan of ten per cent. upon their capital, which would give the State treasury the sum of nearly four millions of dollars. The banks of Worcester also offered the State a loan of three hundred thousand; the Randolph Bank, twenty-five thousand; Columbian Bank, fifty thousand; Revere Bank; fifty thousand; Mount Wollaston Bank, twenty-five thousand; and many other banks throughout the State of proportionate sums. The banks in all the free States tendered heavy loans to the State governments, for the purpose of arming and equipping the troops.

Early on the morning of the seventeenth, the streets of Boston were filled with excited crowds discussing the war news; and awaiting the appearance of the military companies. The most intense enthusiasm was manifested when the Sixth Regiment marched out of the armory of the Second Battalion, at Boylston Hall, and their route to the

13

State House was lined with people. The ladies were out in great numbers, and white handkerchiefs fluttered in the breeze from every point. The State House was the centre of attraction, and a large police force was necessary to keep back the crowd in front and rear. The Sixth Regiment arrived about half past ten o'clock at the State House, and reported for duty. The Washington Guards, Capt. Sampson, also arrived at eleven o'clock, with sixty-eight men, and were attached to the Sixth Regiment.

Previous to the departure of the Sixth Regiment from Boylston Hall, Major B. F. Watson, of Lawrence, addressed the soldiers as follows : —

"Fellow-Soldiers : I have been selected, at a meeting of the commissioned officers of this regiment, to bring to your notice a matter which I am sure will be gratifying to you all. You know of a custom adopted by a New York regiment, and which has prevailed elsewhere, and I know you will be pleased to adopt it. At a meeting of the commissioned officers the subject was mooted, and it was generally agreed that this regimental organization would not be full unless we had a daughter, at this time, when we all have such tender feelings. It was then unanimously agreed, that out of respect and regard for that colonel whom we all esteem so highly, his own daughter, and his only daughter, should be selected. (Loud cheers.) I ask you, fellow-soldiers, to give three cheers for your daughter, Lizzie Clauson Jones."

The men gave three cheers, and the major led the "daughter of the regiment" up and down the line to introduce her, — a pretty little miss, about ten years of age.

Orders were issued on the night of the 16th to the Stoneham Light Infantry to march at once to this city, and report for duty to Col. Jones, of the Sixth Regiment. They arrived about twelve o'clock, under command of

Capt. J. H. Dyke, with seventy-five men, a portion of whom were without guns. The Worcester Light Infantry, Capt. Pratt, which had also been ordered to report to Col. Jones, arrived at one o'clock, with seventy-nine men, a portion of them being without uniforms. All of the companies under Col. Jones changed their old guns for the new rifle muskets, which were sent from the Cambridge Arsenal. They were also furnished with overcoats, knapsacks, blankets, blue woollen drawers, and undershirts and woollen socks. This occupied considerable time, a large number having no military equipments at all.

A new company, raised by Mr. J. P. Richardson, of Cambridge, which was to have joined the Fifth Regiment as Company C, was ordered out, and attached to Colonel Jones' (6th) regiment. They had not been organized, but they promptly answered the call, and a little past ten o'clock sixty of them marched to the State House (Boston) in citizens' dress, without arms, and bearing the American flag. An election of officers was held forthwith. James P. Richardson was chosen captain. They were furnished with equipments, and soon ready for duty.

At three and a half o'clock the regiment, which had been enlarged by the addition of the Washington Guards of Boston, the Worcester Light Infantry, and the Stoneham Light Infantry, making over six hundred men in all, was drawn up in line in Beacon Street, fronting the State House. Col. Jones, with a color-guard, was ordered upon the steps, when Governor Andrew, accompanied by Brigadier-General Butler, Adjutant-General Schouler, the aids of the Governor, and other military men, marched out to meet him. Col. Sargent, senior aid to the Governor, bore the regimental flag.

The Governor said that, as the official representative of the old Commonwealth, he came to bid farewell to this glorious command, previous to their departure on their patriotic mission. They had been summoned, at their country's call, from the quiet associations of business and home, to a solemn and ultimately victorious war. They were called to fight in behalf of the country, its dignity and purity ; in behalf of the flag which had swept the seas in triumph, conveying right and honor all over the world. They were to repair to Washington, which had been built under the direction of " the Father of his country." They had been summoned suddenly; the State government had done all in its power to provide for the necessities of the occasion, and they would bear with them its benefactions and prayers. Those behind cherished them in their heart of hearts, following them with their best wishes, and feeling confident that they would not return until they had done the utmost that patriotic men could do. Here he took the flag, and, after waving it to and fro, amid the applause of the assembled multitude, handed it to Col. Jones.

Col. Jones took the flag, and, saying that he considered it the emblem of everything valuable upon earth, and that it would be so prized by his command, declared that, so help him God, he would never disgrace it.

The regiment then marched to the armory of the Second Battalion, and the men were allowed an hour and a half for rest and supper. At half-past six o'clock they proceeded to the Worcester depot, and took the ears for New York about eight o'clock. An immense crowd surrounded the depot, and cheered the soldiers with great enthusiasm. The following is a list of the officers of this regiment : — Colonel, Edward F. Jones, of Lowell ; Lieutenant-Colonel, Walter Shattuck, of Groton ; Major, Benjamin F. Watson, of Lawrence ; Adjutant, Alpha B. Farr, of Lowell ; Quartermaster, James Monroe, of Cambridge ; Paymaster, Rufus L. Plaisted, of Lowell ; Surgeon, Norman Smith, of Groton ; Chaplain, Charles Babbidge, of Pepperell.

The Davis Guards, of Acton, attached to the Sixth

Regiment, was made up of descendants of the minute-
men who, on the morning of the nineteenth of April,
1775, were the first to march to Concord Bridge to oppose
the British troops.

A rather amusing anecdote is told of the "pop-corn
man." When the Massachusetts Sixth Regiment was drawn
up in line in front of the State House (Boston), he came
round to minister to the wants of the regiment by selling
them his pop-corn. He had not proceeded far, when he
was suddenly overcome by an irresistible feeling of patriotism, threw away his basket, went and enlisted, donned
the uniform, bid his mother a hasty adieu, and left that
night with the Sixth Regiment for the national capital.

The Third Regiment, Colonel D. W. Wardrop, which
was quartered over the Old Colony depot, was ordered to
hold itself in readiness to go by water to Fort Monroe,
Va. A detachment of twenty men, from Plymouth,
arrived, in addition to those which came on the 16th.
The other companies in the regiment were enlarged by
new arrivals and recruits, and the total number was
raised to about two hundred men. They received their
supplies at the State House, in the afternoon, and then
proceeded to Faneuil Hall, where supper was prepared.
At seven o'clock they proceeded to Central Wharf, and
went on board the steamer S. R. Spaulding, Captain Sol-
omon Howes, of the Baltimore line, which had been
chartered to convey the regiment to Fort Monroe. A
crowd was gathered in the vicinity, and received the different companies with loud cheers. The steamer left
shortly after eight o'clock. The following is a list of the
officers of the regiment: — Colonel, David W. Wardrop,
of New Bedford; Lieutenant-Colonel, Charles Raymond,
of Plymouth; Major, John H. Jennings, of New Bedford;
Adjutant, Richard A. Pierce, of New Bedford; Paymaster,
Sandford Almy, of New Bedford; Surgeon, Alexander S.
Holmes, of New Bedford; Surgeon's Mate, Johnson Clark,

13*

of New Bedford ; Chaplain, Thomas E. St. John, of New Bedford.

The Fourth Regiment, Colonel Packard, received an order to proceed to Washington via Fall River route, at half-past six o'clock. It was quartered at Faneuil Hall, where it remained until afternoon.

An order was issued for the discharge of Capt. Sprague, of the Hingham company, in consequence of his failure to respond to the requisition of the Governor, and Luther Stevenson was elected captain. The company was then ordered out, and in the afternoon Capt. Stevenson reported to Col. Packard with forty men. The captain of Company H, Quincy, refused to order out his men, and they chose Thaddeus Newcomb captain. The company reported with twenty men.

The regiment proceeded to the State House in the afternoon, and, after receiving supplies, they marched to the Old Colony depot at seven o'clock, and took the cars for Fall River at eight o'clock. The following is a list of the officers of the regiment : — Colonel, Abner B. Packard, of Quincy ; Lieutenant-Colonel, Hawkes Fearing, Jr., of Hingham ; Major, Hiram C. Alden, of Randolph ; Adjutant, Horace O. Whittemore, of Braintree ; Quartermaster, Othniel Gilmore, of Raynham ; Paymaster, William S. Glover, of Quincy ; Surgeon, Henry M. Saville, of Quincy ; Surgeon's Mate, William D. Atkinson, Jr., of Boston.

Detachments from the New England Guards and the Second Battalion performed escort duty for the regiments which left on the 17th.

The Boston and Maine Railroad Corporation notified Governor Andrew, Governor Washburn, of Maine, and Governor Goodwin, of New Hampshire, that the railroad was open for the transportation of troops of war free of expense.

The citizens of Concord, Mass., subscribed fifteen hundred and seventy-five dollars, on the evening of the seventeenth, to take care of the families of those who had been called into the service of their country.

Only two days had elapsed since the President's proclamation calling for volunteers was issued, and we find three regiments from the " Old Bay State," raised, armed and equipped, and flying over the road, and being borne swiftly on " wind and wave," to the defence of the national capital, and another soon to follow.

Jefferson Davis issued a proclamation inviting applications for letters of marque and reprisal.

Virginia secession ordinance passed in secret session, 60 to 53. Governor Letcher issued a proclamation in which he recognized the independence of the Confederate States.

A large and excited secession meeting was held in Baltimore, Md.

Great Union speech by Gen. Cass, at Detroit, Michigan.

CHAPTER IX.

——————— Though factions rage,
That glorious standard still shall wave,
Hope of the world, through age on age,
And only sink in Freedom's grave.
LUNT.

APRIL 18th. The Eighth Regiment Massachusetts Volunteers, Colonel Munroe, left Boston for Washington, this being the last of the four regiments ordered. Having seen the three depart, great anxiety was manifested by these patriotic men, who were impatiently waiting for the order to start, which was finally given just after dinner.

The line was formed in Merchants' Row shortly before two o'clock, in the presence of an immense crowd. The regiment, as it marched up State Street, was greeted with the greatest enthusiasm by the thousands who were gathered there. It proceeded immediately to the State House, where the ceremony of presenting the flag took place.

The steps, streets, neighboring houses, and in fact every spot where a view of the scene could be had, was crowded. At about half-past three o'clock, the regiment being drawn up in line in Beacon Street, the Governor and aids, accompanied by Gen. Butler, Gen. Schouler and others, went down the steps amid great cheering and waving of handkerchiefs.

The flag was then presented to Colonel Munroe by the Governor, and he spoke as follows: —

"Mr. Commander and Soldiers: — Yesterday you were citizens; to-day you are soldiers. True to the fortunes of your flag, true to the inspirations of your own hearts, true to the undying examples of our fathers, you have hurried up from the towns of Essex, all along from Boston through Marblehead to Cape Ann. Fame to all the men of Massachusetts, to the brave soldiers of a heroic army! You have come to be cradled anew one night in Faneuil Hall, and from breathing once more the inspirations of American liberty, you have hurried forth this afternoon to follow wherever glory leads under the folds of the American banner! (Great applause.) From the bottom of my heart of hearts, standing here as the official representative of Massachusetts, I pay to you, soldiers, citizens, heroes, the homage of my most profound gratitude. And the heart of all Massachusetts beats to-day in sympathy with every word I utter. There is but one sentiment throughout this beautiful domain of liberty. From the shores up to the tall hills of Berkshire, from the beating waves to the granite peaks, it speaks in unison with our common land and our common liberty in deathless echoes. (Applause.)

Soldiers, go forth bearing that flag; —

> " Forever float that standard sheet, —
>   Where breathes the foe but falls before us ?
>   With Freedom's soil beneath our feet,
>   And Freedom's banner streaming o'er us."

(Great applause.)

We stay to defend the hearth-stones of Massachusetts. We remain to guard the homes of the wives and the children of your love; and we swear, whatever fortune may befall you on the field, we will be true to them. (Applause.) I need not say to you, Mr. Commander, that we place entire confidence in your fidelity, courage and ability, in this noble band of men mustered under your command; I need not say that in the gallant son of Massachusetts who stands by my side (Gen. Butler) we have all the confidence which Massachusetts men place in each other. I speak to you not as citizens and soldiers of Massachusetts, but as citizens and soldiers of the American Confederate Union. While we live that Union shall last! (Tumultuous applause.) And until all of us and our posterity have tasted death, the government, the Union of the American people, the heritage of Washington, shall be immortal! (Applause.) Mr. Commander, go forth with the blessing of your country and the confidence of your fellow-citizens. Under the blessing of God, in a good and holy cause, with stout hearts and stalwart arms, go forth to victory! On your shields be returned, or bring them with you. You are the advance guard of Massachusetts soldiers. As such I bid you God speed, and fare you well."

Great applause and cheering followed the Governor's speech, and three cheers were given for General Butler.

General Butler, standing by the side of the Governor, replied : —

" Mr. Commander and Fellow-soldiers : — I desire to say one word to you. We are going to-night upon that duty which the people of this Commonwealth hold as sacred as their dearest wishes. We go to protect the constitutional liberty of the government, the strength of the Union, which under God we will maintain. (Applause.) I have the great pleasure of marching with you, and with you we will give a return to our friends, — to his Excellency who has given us cheering words of encouragement, to the good people of the Commonwealth who are looking for our deeds ; — and indeed, sir, we will make it true, we will either bring back our shields or be brought back upon them. (Applause.) Sons of a Puritan ancestry, believing in the providence of Almighty God, as he was with our fathers, so may he be with us in this strife for the right, for. the good of all, for that great country of human freedom, which if it sinks in blood the liberty of the human race goes out forever. We go to maintain that liberty, and when we prove recreant to that trust, may the God of battles prove our enemy in the hour of our utmost need! Soldiers, we march to-night; and I say for you all, to the good people of Massachusetts, fare you well. We only ask their prayers, we have everything else; and we go forth to say to those who would break down this confederacy, that in this State there is but one sentiment, — " The Union, now and forever, one and inseparable!" (Applause.)

The enthusiasm and excitement were uncontrolled, and cheers without number were given for the regiment, for Gen. Butler, and for the Governor. The line of march was then taken up for Faneuil Hall, and along the whole route the enthusiasm was continuous.

The regiment took final leave of Faneuil Hall shortly before half-past five o'clock, and, preceded by the Brigade Band, proceeded through Merchants' Row, State, Washington and Oak Streets, to the freight depot, No. 2, of the Worcester Railroad, on Albany Street.

On arriving at the depot a detachment of policemen and Lancers kept the crowd out, and the regiment promptly entered the depot and went on board the train. The crowd was immense, and exceeded in numbers that of the day before which gathered to bid farewell to Colonel Jones' regiment, extending for some distance along on each side of the track. As the long train started, at six o'clock, the Brigade Band struck up "Hail Columbia," and the cheering was renewed. The troops thrust their arms out the windows, and many in the crowd shook hands with all whom they could reach.

The scene was more inspiring and exciting than any other we had witnessed in connection with the departure of troops. It was also the largest of the regiments that had left, numbering full eight hundred men.

Brigadier General Butler and staff accompanied the regiment. The following are the regimental officers: — Lieutenant-Colonel, Timothy Munroe, Lynn ; Major, Israel W. Wallis, Beverly ; Adjutant, Edward W. Hinks, Lynn ;

Quartermaster, Samuel T. Payson, Newburyport; Surgeon, David F. Drew, Lynn; Surgeon's Mate, Warren Tapley, Lynn.

The Sixth and Fourth Massachusetts Regiments arrived in New York about sunrise. on the morning of the 18th. One regiment breakfasted at the Astor House and at the St. Nicholas Hotel, and the other at the Metropolitan. At eleven o'clock, after refreshments, they marched down Broadway. They were greeted by cheers and other demonstrations of applause by thousands. Flags floated from every house and store. All the teams, horses and posts had the American flag attached, and nearly every person carried one in his hand. The flag presented by Governor Andrew was cheered the whole length of the route, and "God bless you!" was frequently uttered. Gen. James Appleton, of Ipswich, seventy-six years old, remarked with great emotion, "Those boys won't run. I commanded a regiment of them in the last war." Cheers for the Old Bay State were demanded and enthusiastically given at every step. They marched to the Jersey ferry, where there was a perfect ovation. The Sixth embarked at twelve o'clock, and took the train direct for Washington. They arrived at Jersey City at twenty minutes past twelve o'clock, and were received with the wildest demonstrations of enthusiasm. As the train left the depot, cheer on cheer rent the air, and many were the promises made to them that "Three thousand Jersey Blues would be with the sons of the Old Bay State in one week's time, to show their loyalty to the Constitution and the Union."

From the public buildings and private dwellings floated the stars and stripes. Three times three cheers were given in honor of the Old Bay State, that she was the first in the field.

They arrived at Philadelphia in the early part of the evening, took supper at the Continental Hotel, and were quartered for the night mainly at the Girard House. The cheering was incessant along the route.

Harper's Ferry arsenal was destroyed by Lieut. Jones, to prevent its falling into the hands of the secessionists. Lieut. Jones and his command of forty-three men made their escape. He says, as the federal troops at Harper's Ferry rushed across the Potomac bridge, the people rushed into the arsenal, and he believes a large number perished, as repeated explosions occurred. He saw the light of the burning buildings many miles in his retreat. The lieutenant, having been advised that a force of twenty-five hundred troops were ordered by the Governor to take possession of Harper's Ferry, and finding his position untenable, under the direction of the War Department he destroyed all the munitions of war, the armory, arsenal and buildings. He withdrew his command under the cover of night, and almost in the presence of twenty-five hundred troops. He lost three men, taken by the rebels. Fifteen thousand stand of arms were destroyed. His command made a forced march of thirty miles, from Harper's Ferry to Hagerstown, Md. They were enthusiastically received.

Governor Hicks, of Maryland, issued a proclamation, assuring the people that no troops would be sent from that State, unless it was for the defence of the national capital.

April 19th. The Massachusetts Sixth Regiment was assailed by a mob in its passage through Baltimore en route for Washington. Two Massachusetts soldiers killed, and several wounded, — the first blood shed in the "Rebellion of 1861." The nineteenth of April, the anniversary of the battle of Lexington and Concord, — that evermemorable day in our nation's history. The first American Revolution was inaugurated by Massachusetts blood on the nineteenth of April, 1775, and the second American revolution was inaugurated by Massachusetts blood on the nineteenth of April, 1861.

14

Eighty-six years ago couriers were sent through the towns and villages of Middlesex County to rouse the people in resistance to British tyranny. On this nineteenth of April, 1861, also, couriers were sent through the same district to call out the Fifth and Seventh Regiments, and were received with the ringing of bells, the firing of cannon, and the assembling of soldiers as brave, true and prompt, as those of the olden time.

On the morning of the nineteenth, at the President Street depot of the Philadelphia Railroad, in Baltimore, an immense crowd assembled, in anticipation of the arrival of a large number of troops from New York and Massachusetts. Shortly after eleven o'clock the train from Philadelphia, comprising twenty-nine cars, arrived at the depot. Without disembarking the soldiers from the train, the several cars had horses attached, and about nine were drawn along Pratt Street to the Camden station, the first six without any marked objection. For some reason the horses attached to the seventh car became restive, and were taken from the car at the Pratt Street bridge, and the car moved without their aid to within a short distance of Gay Street, between Gay and Frederick Street. A number of laborers were engaged in repairing the bed of the street, and just at the moment the car reached Gay Street they were engaged in removing the cobble stones from the principal portion of the street. Some thirty or forty men assembled at this point, having followed the car from the depot, and, with cheers for Davis and the confederacy, hurled bitter taunts at the Northern Black Republicans, as they termed them.

This continued for several minutes. When the horses were again attached and the car moved off, it was proposed to stone it. Before the car had gone twenty yards almost every window was broken, and a portion of the crowd followed, hurling paving-stones.

The eighth car was treated in the same manner, but the ninth car, apparently being empty, or at least no person being visible, escaped only with one stone. The crowd exulted in their work, exclaiming that Black Republicans should not pass through Maryland. A lapse of five minutes succeeded, a number of respectable persons meanwhile urging the crowd to tear up the track. After the first train passed, one was observed on the Pratt Street bridge, when the anchors were dragged on the track at the corner of Gay Street, and part of the track taken up. Observing this, the cars were turned back to President Street depot, and the troops disembarked and prepared to march through the streets. Mayor Brown with a number of police appeared at their head and led the way. They came away at a brisk pace, and when they reached Centre Market Square, an immense concourse of people closed in behind them, and commenced stoning them. When they reached Gay Street, where the track had been taken up, a large crowd of men, armed with paving-stones, showered them on their heads with such force that several of them were knocked down in the ranks. After lying a few minutes they crowded into the stores on Pratt Street. At the corner of South and Pratt Streets, a man fired a pistol into the ranks of the militia, when those in the rear ranks immediately wheeled and fired upon their assailants, and several were wounded. The guns of the soldiers that had fallen wounded were seized and fired upon the ranks with fatal effect. In two or three instances, after reaching Culvert Street, the troops succeeded in checking their pursuers by rapid fire, which brought down two or three, and were not much molested until they reached Howard Street, where another large crowd was assembled. Some stones were thrown at them, but their guns were not loaded, and they passed on, through a dense crowd, down Howard Street towards the depot.

The scene on Pratt Street was of a most startling character; the wounded soldiers, three in number, were taken up carefully, and carried to places of safety by citizens. Along the street at the Camden station, where trains leave for Washington, there was assembled a large detachment of police under direction of Marshal Kane. It soon appeared that orders were given to clear the tracks near the main depot building. This was done, and soon after a large passenger car of the Philadelphia Railroad came up at a rapid rate, filled with soldiers. This car was soon followed by about sixteen more, all occupied by troops. Upon inquiry it was ascertained they consisted of the Sixth Regiment of Massachusetts Infantry, in all eleven companies, with an aggregate of eight hundred and sixty men.

As soon as the train arrived, some of the troops were compelled to change cars, when they were hooted at by the crowd, which made no overt act. Several young men appeared at one of the cars and displayed revolvers, whereupon the captain of one of the companies drew his sword and declared he would protect his men. Many expected the train would start immediately, but it did not move until half-past twelve, a delay being occasioned by the fact that President Garrett had received information that a large crowd of excited men had determined to tear up the track and blow up the bridges, and thereby prevent the passage of the trains.

In a few minutes after the train left, a discharge of firearms attracted the attention of the crowd to the corner of Pratt and Howard Streets, where a body of infantry from one of the Northern States, about one hundred and fifty strong, was seen rapidly approaching the depot, and no doubt anxious to reach the cars. The excitement was beyond description, and a man displaying a flag of the Confederate States seemed to be the rallying point for the people. Some assaulted the infantry with stones, when a number of the latter discharged their muskets. At least twenty shots were fired, but as far as learned no person was injured. Whilst they were entering the cars, a crowd of young men gave them several volleys of bricks and stones, some of which demolished a car window, whereupon three or four muskets were pointed through the car windows and fired, but no one was injured. The train with the second detachment left at a quarter past one, being stoned as they left.

The city was in tremendous excitement. Martial law was proclaimed, and the military rushed to their armories. Parties were roaming the streets armed with guns and pistols. Stores closed and business suspended. Everybody in a state of dread. A party of the mob rushed into the telegraph office and cut the wires, but they were soon repaired. Squads paraded the streets, fully armed, on the lookout for military from the North. A town meeting was called in Monument Square, at four o'clock in the afternoon, which was attended by an immense crowd. The State flag was hoisted. Mayor Brown said he was opposed to the call of the President, in spirit and object, but as Maryland was still in the Union, he had exerted himself to his utmost ability to protect the passage of troops through the city. He, however, felt that this should not be, and had telegraphed to the President urging that no more troops be sent through.

Gov. Hicks was sent for, and said he was opposed to secession, but the right of revolution could not be disputed.

Speeches were made by Messrs. Teakle, Wallis, W. P. Preston and others, justifying the people of Baltimore, and declaring that no Northern troops should invade their soil to subjugate and make war on their brethren of the South.

Late in the evening, General Butler telegraphed Governor Andrew the intelligence of his own arrival, with

14*

the command of Col. Munroe, at Philadelphia; confirming the rumor that Col. Jones had been attacked in the streets of Baltimore, that two Massachusetts men were killed, and several wounded, and adds, — "Troops fought manfully. No man offered to run. They bore the attack with the utmost patience, until prominent citizens of Baltimore told them to fire. They did so. Part of the mob responded with fire, the rest scattered. All have arrived at Washington except six injured, who are well cared for at Baltimore."

A dispatch from Washington, April 19, says: —

"The Massachusetts troops arrived this evening, and are quartered in the Capitol. Several of them were wounded in Baltimore and sent to the infirmary, while others who were less injured in that city are on duty with their comrades."

At half-past two o'clock, A. M., the following dispatch was sent by His Excellency the Governor to the Mayor of Baltimore: —

EXECUTIVE DEPARTMENT, COUNCIL CHAMBER,
BOSTON, April 20, 1861.

" *To His Honor the Mayor:* — I pray you to cause the bodies of our Massachusetts soldiers dead in Baltimore to be immediately laid out, preserved with ice, and tenderly sent forward by express to me. All expenses will be paid by this Commonwealth.

"JOHN A. ANDREW,

"Governor of Massachusetts."

At half-past nine o'clock, A. M., after a correspondence between the Governor and Messrs. Gardner Brewer & Co. of this city, which reflects honor on the intelligent benevolence of that firm, they sent the following dispatch to their correspondents in Baltimore: —

" *Messrs. Mills, Mayhew & Co., Baltimore:*

"We telegraph to you at the request and in behalf of

Governor Andrew of this State. Will you co-operate with the Mayor of Baltimore in securing respectful treatment to the corpses of our dead soldiers, and their being carefully forwarded packed in ice, and particularly we wish you to secure the very best medical attendance and careful nursing to our wounded. We will be responsible to you for all expenses. Nurses can be sent from here if desired.   GARDNER BREWER & Co."

At noon the following answer was received from Messrs. Mills, Mayhew & Co : —

" We have your telegram, and will attend carefully to your instructions. Nothing is wanted which we cannot furnish."

At two o'clock, P. M., this answer was received by the Governor from the Mayor : —

"*Hon. John A. Andrew, Governor of Massachusetts :*

" SIR : — No one deplores the sad events of yesterday in this city more deeply than myself, but they were inevitable. Our people viewed the passage of armed troops to another State through the streets as an invasion of our soil, and could not be restrained. The authorities exerted themselves to the best of their ability, but with only partial success. Governor Hicks was present, and concurs in all my views as to the proceedings now necessary for our protection.

" When are these scenes to be ceased ? Are we to have a war of sections ! God forbid !

" The bodies of the Massachusetts soldiers could not be sent on to Boston as you requested, all communication between this city and Philadelphia by railroad and with Boston steamers having ceased ; but they have been placed in cemented coffins, and will be placed with proper funeral ceremonies in the mausoleum of Green Mount Cemetery, where they shall be retained until further directions are received from you.　The wounded are tenderly cared for.　I appreciate your offer, but Baltimore will claim it as her right to pay all expenses incurred.

"Very respectfully,

"Your obedient servant,

"GEO. WM. BROWN,

"Mayor of Baltimore."

To this the following reply was returned by the Governor:—

"*To His Honor George Wm. Brown, Mayor of Baltimore:*

"DEAR SIR:—I appreciate your kind attention to our wounded and our dead, and trust that at the earliest moment the remains of our fallen will return to us.

"I am overwhelmed with surprise that a peaceful march of American citizens over the highway to the defence of our common Capitol should be deemed aggressive by Baltimoreans.　Through New York the march was triumphal.

"JOHN A. ANDREW, Governor of Massachusetts."

Of the citizens of Baltimore, there were seven killed and many wounded.　Mr. R. W. Davis was shot dead near the Camden station; the others killed were John Mc-Ghan, Sebastian Gies, Patrick Clark, B. Thomas Miles, Wm. C. Maloney, W. Reed.　Wounded, Patrick Griffin, fatally, others unknown.

The Massachusetts soldiers killed in Baltimore were A. O. Whitney and Luther C. Ladd, of Lowell.

Wounded and left in Baltimore — Sergeant Ames of the Lowell City Guards, slightly; private E. Coburn, of the same place, shot in the head, not fatal; private Michael Green of Lawrence, slightly; S. H. Needham, skull fractured (since died); another, name unknown, at the infirmary, badly wounded; H. W. Danforth and Edward Cooper were shot in the thigh; also Capt. J. H. Dike, of

Company C., Stoneham Light Infantry, received a ball wound in the head, and was left at Baltimore.

The following are the names of the wounded who proceeded on to Washington: —

Company C, Stoneham Light Infantry. Henry Dyke, ball wound in the leg.

W. H. Young, hit by a brickbat on the head.

Stephen Flanders, bad wound on the head by a brickbat.

H. Perry, wounded on the knee by brickbat.

John Fostier, wounded on the head with a stone.

C. G. Gill, bad wound on the knee from the breech of a gun.

Joshua W. Pennall, knocked in the head by a brickbat.

John Kempton, several bad bruises on the legs and arms from paving stones.

Morris Meade, wounded in the leg by a brickbat.

Lieut. James Rowe, two side cuts in the head from brickbats.

Daniel Brown, third finger of the left hand shot off.

Company D, Lowell. C. H. Chandler, wounded in the head by a brick. (Pop-corn man.)

Company I, Lawrence. V. G. Gingrass, shot through the arm.

Alonzo Joy, two fingers shot off.

Sergeant G. J. Dorall, cut on the head with a brickbat.

Company D. W. H. Samson, struck in the eye and on the back of the head with paving stones, with other severe bruises on the body.

Charles Stinson of Company C, of Lowell, had nose broken with a brick.

Company D. Ira W. Moore, badly wounded on left arm with brickbat.

Geo. Alexander, back of the head and neck badly cut with a brick.

The names of the brave soldiers who fell in this heroic

expedition will stand on our nation's history parallel with those of the Revolution, and be immortalized with the sacred memories which cluster around the men of Concord and Lexington.

It is stated that one of the Massachusetts soldiers who was mortally wounded and bled to death, while in the last struggles stood erect, raised his right hand toward heaven, and exclaimed, — " *All hail to the stars and stripes!* " and instantly expired.

April 21.   Thus far it appears that the Sixth Regiment, under Col. Jones, has arrived in Washington, forcing its way through Baltimore.   The Fourth Regiment under Col. Packard, and the Third under Col. Wardrop, were safely landed at Fortress Monroe.   The Eighth Regiment under Col. Munroe of Lynn, accompanied by Brig. General Butler, has reached Annapolis, by steamers from Philadelphia, en route for Washington, the railway communication having been temporarily interrupted.

Having followed them to their destination, we leave them here, and take a general survey of the whole country.

A diabolical attempt was made to poison the Fourth Regiment while on board the " State of Maine " at New York, previous to leaving for Fortress Monroe, on the eighteenth, by sending poisoned brandy on board.   One died, and four or five others suffered very much from its influence, but recovered.   The perpetrator of the outrage is unknown.

April 19th.   The President issued a proclamation ordering the blockade of the ports of South Carolina, Georgia, Alabama, Florida, Mississippi, Louisiana and Texas, and declaring that if any person, acting under the pretended authority of said States, shall molest a vessel of the United States, or the persons or cargo on board, such person shall be deemed guilty of piracy.

General Scott issued an order extending the military

department of Washington so as to include the District of Columbia and the States of Maryland, Delaware and Pennsylvania, and appointing Major-General Patterson to the command.

Governor Hicks, of Maryland, and Mayor Brown, of Baltimore, informed the President that it was not possible for soldiers to pass through Baltimore unless they fought their way. President Lincoln replied that no more troops would pass through the city for the present, provided they were allowed to pass armed around the city unmolested.

The city council of Philadelphia appropriated one million dollars to equip volunteers and support their families.

Governor Buckingham, of Connecticut, issued a proclamation calling for the Second Regiment of volunteers. Fourteen thousand dollars were subscribed at Norwich, for the families of volunteers.

Rhode Island Marine Artillery arrived in New York with six pieces of artillery, and left same day for Washington. Governor Hicks, of Maryland, telegraphed Governor Sprague, of Rhode Island, as follows: —

Governor Hicks to Governor Sprague: — " I understand you are about to proceed to Washington with the Rhode Island regiment. I advise you not to take them through Baltimore, and thus save trouble."

Governor Sprague to Governor Hicks: — " The Rhode Island Regiment are going to fight, and it matters not whether they fight in Baltimore or Washington."

The war feeling was increasing. New companies were concentrating. Seventeen hundred volunteers, from Ohio, arrived in Pittsburg, Pa., en route for Washington. From Springfield, Ill., we learn that forty-nine companies had been accepted, and tenders of as many more had been made. All the railroad companies of the State had volunteered to carry accepted companies to the place of rendezvous free of charge.

In Chicago, two thousand men had signed the muster-roll. The Zouave regiment was fast filling up, and the enthusiasm was intense.

A dispatch from Harrisburg, Pa., April 18th, says : — "A large number of companies have arrived, and the camp, forming a mile above the city, is alive with excitement to-night. The whole population are in the streets. Two companies are quartered in the legislative halls. There will be eight thousand troops here by Saturday. Every train brings hundreds. A special messenger has been sent to Washington for arms."

It will be remembered that only three days have elapsed since the President issued his proclamation calling for troops. A correspondent writes from Washington, under date April 19th : — "Twenty-four companies, averaging one hundred men, have already been mustered into the service of the government. Five hundred Pennsylvania troops arrived this afternoon. Several were hurt with stones while passing through Baltimore. They are quartered in the Capitol.

"The old hall of the House of Representatives, where Clay, Adams, Webster, Calhoun, McDuffie and hundreds of others, eminent in public life, deliberated, is now turned into barracks. Company E (Washington) are quartered in the handsome room on Revolutionary Claims. Two of the Pennsylvania companies are quartered in the luxurious committee-rooms of the north wing. The soldiers had Brussels carpets, marble wash-stands, and all that sort of thing, but seemed to think they should prefer to all this to have a bite of something to eat, as they had tasted nothing since a hasty early breakfast at Harrisburg. They had suffered, too, miserably from thirst on the way, and, at one station where they stopped, were glad to quench their thirst in a pool of muddy water standing in a field. This, with the hostile reception received at Baltimore, gave them a pretty rude taste of soldiers' life.

They took all in good spirits, except the failure in the commissariat department at their quarters. Some bacon sides had been served out in the basement (Senate kitchen refectory), where a fire had been started, and some of the soldiers were struggling, with a dull knife, to chip off a rasher, but nothing seemed to be in readiness for the hungry men."

In New York city all classes were aroused. The First Regiment of Zouaves bound themselves by a solemn oath to march through Baltimore.

On the 19th the Trinity Church steeple was graced with a starry flag, amidst the uproarious cheers of thousands in Broadway and Wall Streets. The chimes pealed out the "Star-Spangled Banner" and "Hail Columbia."

The celebrated Seventh Regiment, of New York, Col. Lefferts, numbering nine hundred and ninety-one men, left New York for Washington. They received a continuous ovation all through New Jersey. Cannon were fired and houses illuminated. They reached Philadelphia late at night. The streets were alive with people to witness their arrival. They proceeded on their way, and arrived at Annapolis on the 21st, where they were joined by the Massachusetts Eighth, with Gen. Butler.

Early on the morning of the 24th, the New York Seventh and Massachusetts Eighth Regiments marched from Annapolis, and arrived at the Junction, a distance of nineteen miles, at ten o'clock on the morning of the 25th, and, at four o'clock in the afternoon, left in the train for Washington.

To give those of our readers who have never witnessed such a scene some faint idea of the hasty greetings and hurried farewells immediately preceding the departure of a regiment, we subjoin the following from a New York paper. It may provoke a smile, and serve to lighten a dark picture.

"At about a quarter to three o'clock a general hurry

15

and movement throughout the rooms indicated that the time for muster was near at hand.   The officers moved faster and seemed more preoccupied.   Col. Lefferts bluntly declined the offer of an escort from the Zouave corps, on the ground that it should have been made before, and that he had now no time to arrange for it.   Recruits were told that it was too late to consider their cases now, and that they must report at some volunteer station. The members began to file off into their company rooms, from which outsiders were now excluded.   Tardy arrivals were greeted enthusiastically, in the same spirit that the Biblical shepherd rejoiced more over the one sheep he imagined lost than over the flocks he had safely penned. 'Why, here's Pete!' 'I thought you wasn't coming;' 'Bully for you, old buffer!' were the rough welcomes shouted to new-comers.   Yonder are a party of friends, some of whom are to go with the regiment, while the others stay at home, and you may hear the request,— 'Kill one of the scoundrels for me, Billy;' the advice, 'Take care of yourself, old fellow, and I'll see to things at home;' the promise, 'I'll come back promoted, father, or I won't come back at all;' and then, in a woman's voice, 'God bless you! I shall think of you and pray for you all the time.   It's very hard to, but'— and then a few tears, low whisperings and a kiss.   The most thoughtless began to grow serious now, and the most frivolous became earnest and anxious.

" Then, as the soldiers began to engage more in conversation with each other, various interesting circumstances in connection with their departure began to be mentioned. Here were several post-office clerks, who had been granted leave of absence, with full pay, for the war ; clerks in various mercantile houses had the same leave, with the same conditions.   A Mr. Murphy had sent two sons and two employees with the Seventh, and armed them with fine revolvers.   Other soldiers had been presented with revolvers, also, and a general display of five and six-shooters ensued. This man had been married only two days before, but his wife said ' Go,' and he came. Another was engaged to be married on Sunday, but the wedding was postponed three months, that he might serve his country. ' I may die a bachelor yet, you know,' he lightly remarked, as he told of the circumstances. ' I haven't had time to arrange my business, for I only received notice that we should move at ten o'clock, to-day,' remarked another, ' but I'm here, my hearties.' ' I wonder will all the boys turn out?' said a sergeant; ' a day and a half is short work, eh?' ' By George,' laughed another, adjusting his sword-belt, ' I came up here to bid you good-by, but I couldn't stand it, so I jumped into these things, and will go along. Didn't have much time to bid the folks farewell you bet.' ' What do you think the Governor said to me?' asked a young recruit; ' why, he said "Remember Sumter!" and said he'd like to go too.' ' That's like Fan,' shouted another; ' she said she'd go if she were a man. Do you think I'd back out after that?' ' How are you, my boy? You didn't back out, did you?' Then a long shake-hands, and the response, ' Nor I didn't want to.' ' Here's a bouquet Mollie sent. Look at that, — " May peace soon bring you back to me." ' ' Mother gave me this little flag. God bless her! I'll never disgrace it.' ' What do you think of that for a badge? (displaying a beautifully-worked rosette); that goes over my heart.' Breaking up these conversations there came, every once in a while, cheers upon cheers for the Seventh and for the Union, and snatches of national songs, shouted with hearty, untremulous voices."

On the 20th the Virginia secessionists, in Richmond, had a great rejoicing over the fall of Fort Sumter. They claim to have had three thousand in procession, hoisted the Southern Confederacy flag, fired a hundred guns, and had exulting speeches from Governor Letcher, Attorney-General Tucker, and other magnates.   On motion of John M. Patton, they enthusiastically

" *Resolved*, That we rejoice with high, exultant, heartfelt joy at the triumph of the Southern Confederacy over the accursed government at Washington in the capture of Fort Sumter."

Many of the houses were brilliantly illuminated from attic to cellar; flags of the Southern Confederacy were abundantly displayed from roofs and windows; the streets blazed with bonfires; the sky lighted with showers of pyrotechnics; and, until midnight, crowd after crowd found speakers to address them from balconies and street-corners.

An immense meeting, called by Virginia citizens at Mobile, took place on the 18th, with great enthusiasm and rejoicing over the secession of Virginia.   At Montgomery, same day, a meeting of the Virginians, Louisianians, Tennesseeans and Kentuckians was held, to rejoice over the glorious news from Virginia.   One hundred guns were fired, the city illuminated, and general joy expressed that the revolution was complete.   Nearly all the naval officers of Virginia had sent in their resignations to Washington.   The confederate flag was raised at Point of Rocks, in Maryland, on the 19th.   The rebellion in Virginia was formidable.   Northern men, with their families, were expelled, leaving everything, narrowly escaping with their lives.   So bitter was the feeling against them that many were compelled to leave for expressing Union sentiments.

Governor Dennison, of Ohio, appointed Capt. George B. McClellan, formerly of the army, major-general and commander-in-chief of the Ohio State troops.   This gentleman is a graduate of West Point, served with marked distinction during the Mexican war, and was one of three officers sent by our government to watch the campaign at the Crimea.

Steamship Star of the West captured by rebels, under Col. Van Dorn, off Indianola, and taken to New Orleans as a prize to the Confederate States.

April 20th.   A mob from Baltimore destroyed the railroad bridges on the line to Philadelphia.   All the bridges between Baltimore and Havre de Grace were destroyed or rendered useless.   The trains on the night of the 20th went through safely to the bridge at Canton (three miles from Baltimore), where a crowd lying in wait fired pistols at the engineer, who stopped the train. The crowd compelled the passengers to leave the cars, and, taking possession of them, forced the engineer to take them back to the Gunpowder River bridge.   Here the train stopped.   The crowd set fire to the draw of the bridge, and remained until that portion was burnt.   They then returned to the Bush River bridge, and set the draw on fire.   Next they went to the Canton bridge and burned that.   The train then conveyed its passengers to Baltimore.

A body of carpenters and workmen, armed, were sent from Harrisburg to repair the bridges on the Northern and Central Road, which, conjointly with men sent from Philadelphia, and some Massachusetts soldiers, soon put the road in good order.

Gosport Navy Yard, opposite Norfolk, Va., was burned by United States officers, to prevent its falling into the hands of the secessionists.   United States ships Pennsylvania, seventy-four guns; Delaware, seventy-four; Columbus, seventy-four; steam-frigate Merrimac, forty-four; frigate Raritan, forty-four; frigate Columbia, forty-four; sloop Germantown, twenty-two; sloop Plymouth, twenty-two; brig Dolphin, eight; and the frigate United States (in ordinary), in the harbor, were scuttled and set on fire.   The value of property destroyed is estimated at fifty million dollars.

The steamer Yankee reports arrived at Norfolk, on the

15*

afternoon of the 17th, and, finding a movement afloat to seize her, proceeded to the navy yard and placed herself under the guns of the yard.

On the 18th the custom-house officers came to seize her, but the commander of the yard refused to yield her.

On the 20th the Pawnee, under Commodore Paulding, arrived at Fort Monroe, took aboard the Third Massachusetts Regiment, and proceeded to the navy yard, where the officers had commenced destroying the public property to prevent its falling into the hands of the enemy.

They had scuttled all the ships, the Cumberland being the only one in commission; they cut down the shears, &c. Preparations were made to make demolition complete.

The Pawnee, with the Cumberland in tow, assisted by the Yankee, started, and, after passing the navy yard, sent up a signal rocket, when a match was applied, and in an instant ships, ship-houses and store-houses were in flames.

So rapid were the flames that Commander Rogers, of the navy, and Captain Wright, of the engineers, were unable to reach the point of rendezvous, where a boat was waiting for them, and were left behind. Large quantities of provisions, cordage, machinery, and buildings of great value, were destroyed. The burning of the navy yard was done by Union men, who were in the majority, but comparatively unarmed.

When the Pawnee came up, the Cumberland and Merrimac lay broadside to, their guns loaded, thinking she was in the hands of the rebels. Similar opinion prevailed on board the Pawnee, and she was ready for action. The cheering aboard the vessels and on shore showed how satisfactory was the answer to our hail from the Cumberland, that she was the United States steamer Pawnee.

The Union men employed in the navy yard cut down the flag-staff so that it could not be used by the rebels. The guns in the navy yard were spiked.

The following letter from a private in the New Bedford company at Fort Monroe, describing the part he took in the destruction of the Norfolk navy-yard property, will be read with interest. The writer is well known, a rising lawyer of ability, and distinguished for his many virtues of character and patriotism: —

" And so, brother ——, I am a soldier, and have already encountered a soldier's dangers. Let my enlistment and the journey here pass. Suffice it to say that I arrived here on Saturday, about eleven, A. M. . . . We were exhausted with poor fare, sea-sickness, want of sleep, and bad air. We expected to remain here and defend this fort. At about five in the afternoon, as we were expecting quarters and a good night's sleep, we were summoned into line, and ordered to the Norfolk navy yard, which was in immediate danger ; and we were to defend it against the Virginians, or retake it if it had been captured by the Southern troops collected there. We had about a hundred regulars, the marines of the Pawnee. We, undisciplined and ill-conditioned as we were, went on board the Pawnee, just from Charleston. We trod for the first time a man-of-war — and her guns looked deathly. Our friends of the Fourth Regiment felt that they should see few of us again. We received our twenty-five cartridges and percussion caps apiece, and loaded our guns without putting the caps on. At or near Norfolk, we passed the frowning batteries of the secessionists. The marines had the cannon pushed forward, all ready to return a fire at any moment. . Hot shot from the batteries could have sunk us ; but they did not open, and we went safely on.

" We approached the navy yard about half-past eight in the evening. We were serious, but calm, and were ready for a fight. I held my percussion cap in my hand. We knew not whether the navy yard was in possession of our friends or enemies. But we found that it was still ours. As we came within almost pistol-shot of the Cum-

berland there, our boatswain saw that her men were just
applying the matches to guns which would rake our bow,
where our company was. If they had fired, our company
would have been destroyed. She had mistaken our
signal, and thought we were secessionists. Our boatswain cried out, again, 'Pawnee! United States ship!'
and the mistake was discovered in time, and the men of
the Cumberland, and also of the Pennsylvania, gave us a
round of cheers, and their bands played 'Hail Columbia.'
We disembarked, and at once were set to rolling several
thousand shells and balls into the sea and laying powder
trains ; while the marines spiked or otherwise disabled the
cannon in the yard. We went on board about half-past
twelve o'clock at night, but the Pawnee did not leave till
four o'clock in the morning.

"Soon after we left, the powder trains exploded; the
vessels, three or four of which we left behind, and the
buildings, were all in a blaze, lighting the sea for a long
distance. This loss of the munitions of war to Virginia is
immense. On our return we passed the batteries, which
we expected the exasperated Virginians would fire upon
us, and the marines stood at their guns. The commander said we should have a warm time. Still, we were so
exhausted, that we even lay down to sleep. The marines
told us they did not see how we could sleep when we
were likely to be sunk at any moment. For some reasons
which we do not know, the batteries did not open on us,
and we were happily preserved. Our men were calm,
and for my own part, I felt only a little different from
what I should in doing a responsible piece of law business.

"It is singular to witness the elasticity of human nature,
which adapts itself to almost anything. There was something almost sublime in the stoicism of the regulars.
While we were at Norfolk the secessionists sunk vessels
in the channel to prevent our return. They were under
the direction of a Virginian, late a lieutenant in the ser-

vice of the United States. We, however, passed through. We got back to the fort at about six o'clock, on Sunday forenoon. We were gladly welcomed by our friends of the Third Regiment, who expected to find our ranks thinned. Some of them hardly dared to meet us, expecting to find that many had fallen."

John C. Breckenridge made a great speech at Louisville, Ky., denouncing the government. A great mass-meeting was held in New York. All parties for the Union. The United States arsenal at Liberty, Mo., was seized by rebels.

On the 20th, Governor Andrew received a dispatch from Brigadier-General Butler, requesting him to forward more troops, arms, and ammunition, as speedily as possible, in order that they could force a passage through to Washington. Active measures were immediately taken to comply with the request, and a special order was issued calling out the Light Artillery, in addition to the companies composing the Fifth Regiment.

The Somerville Light Infantry (Co. B, Fifth Regiment), Capt. Brastow, arrived, and proceeded to Faneuil Hall, where the Fifth Regiment was quartered. The company was composed of fine-looking men, and when they passed down State Street the crowd of spectators applauded heartily.

The Mechanic Light Infantry, of Salem (Co. B, Seventh Regiment), Capt. George H. Pierson, and the Salem City Guard (Co. H, Seventh Regiment), Capt. Henry F. Danforth, having been detailed to join the Fifth Regiment, left Salem in an extra train at nine o'clock on Saturday morning. Previous to their departure a beautiful silk flag was presented to the Mechanic Light Infantry by Perley Putnam, a veteran eighty-four years of age, and a former commander of the corps. The city government of Salem voted $15,000 for the benefit of the families of the volunteers.

The companies arrived at the Eastern Railroad depot, Boston, about ten o'clock, and marched to Faneuil Hall, where the commanders reported for duty to Col. Lawrence.

Every endeavor was made to have the regiment properly equipped and on the road by six o'clock in the afternoon; but it was found impossible to have the overcoats and under-garments in readiness before midnight. The Light Artillery, Major Cook, were ready to start very soon after receiving the order, with about one hundred and twenty men. The horses necessary for the company, seventy in number, were purchased of the Metropolitan Railroad Corporation. The full battery, six brass six-pounders, together with the horses, ten tons of powder, and a large quantity of shot, were sent on a train, at ten o'clock in the evening, to New York. At about half-past one o'clock the artillery company marched to the Worcester Railroad depot, and took their places in the train, where they waited until the Fifth Regiment arrived. About five o'clock, refreshments, in the shape of baked beans, were served to each man; and after they got through they amused themselves by throwing the plates out of the windows of the cars and smashing them.

The Fifth Regiment were not able to get all of their equipments until a very late hour. At four o'clock the different companies were ordered up, and, after receiving their rations, the regimental line was formed, and they marched to the Worcester depot. A large crowd was assembled to see them off, notwithstanding the unseasonable hour. The artillery company started in a train by themselves at about six o'clock, and the Fifth Regiment started about half an hour later. They were joined at Worcester by the Third Battalion of Rifles, Major T. E. Devens.

On the night of the 20th, at the solemn hour of midnight, the writer of this work, in company with a gentleman friend, accompanied an anxious mother to take another look of her darling son, who was one of Major Cook's artillerists, and who was to leave that night. All was still and quiet save here and there the rapid footfall of a soldier or perhaps two, hurrying to their place of rendezvous, their bright arms glittering in the moonlight, or now and then the clattering of hoofs with a solitary carriage conveying some friends of soldiers to " see them once more," before they departed. No noise or confusion indicated to us the place of their meeting. We wended our way to the State House. All was silent, — no signs of life. We passed around to the back entrance, where stood a solitary carriage waiting for some officers who were in council with the governor in the executive chamber. A sentinel, pacing to and fro, demanded to know our business. On being informed, he gave us all necessary information as to where· the troops could be found. We proceeded hastily to the " armory," in the lower part of the city. On arriving there, we found congregated an immense mass of human beings anxiously waiting for the soldiers to come out, as there was " no admittance " inside. As soon as it was known that ladies were in waiting, an officer came out, and our gentleman attendant told him our business, and asked him if we could go in. He replied, " Oh, yes; I'll take the ladies in, but I can't take you in." A signal rap, and the door was opened just sufficient to crowd through, and immediately closed after us. And such a scene ! The soldiers were amusing themselves in every imaginable " innocent " way. Some were stretched on benches to get a few moments' rest ; some were talking and laughing ; others seemed sober and thoughtful ; while in one corner of the room a company of a dozen or more were singing " Dixie " at the top of their voices, which had scarcely ended when a crowd in another part of the room struck up

" I am going home to die no more."

We found the object of our search, and after a few moments' conversation we took an affectionate farewell of him and hurried to our homes.

Early on the morning of the 21st they left Boston for the seat of war.

April 21. Steamers Baltic, with the New York Twelfth Regiment, the R. R. Cuyler, with the Eleventh, the Columbia, with the Sixth Regiment on board, accompanied by the Harriet Lane, with sealed orders, left New York at six o'clock in the evening.

The regiments marched down Broadway about one o'clock, embarking at two o'clock. The scene on Broadway and at the piers defies description. Probably from four to five hundred thousand people witnessed their departure, perfectly wild with joyful and patriotic enthusiasm, though tinctured with sorrow by relatives.

The Rhode Island regiment, under command of Governor Sprague, one thousand strong, arrived in the morning, and left in the Coalzacoalcos at sundown.

The harbor was the scene of great excitement as the fleet left. All the piers, landings, and house-tops in New York, Jersey City, Hoboken, and Brooklyn, and the Battery, were crowded with people, and thousands of boats filled with people saluted them as they steamed down the bay. Flags were dipped, cannons roared, bells rang, and steam-whistles shrilly saluted, and thousands sent up cheers of parting.

Over four thousand men left New York on that day for the seat of war. From this date, for many days, troops were rapidly pouring in for Washington, Annapolis, and Fortress Monroe.

The United States Branch Mint at Charlotte, N. C., was seized by the rebels.

April 22. Governor Hicks sent a communication to the President, urging the withdrawal of troops from Maryland, a cessation of hostilities, and a reference of the national dispute to the arbitrament of Lord Lyons. Secretary (of State) Seward replied, that the troops must pass through Maryland, and that our troubles could not be " referred to any foreign arbitrament."

General Robert G. Lee was appointed by the Virginia convention " commander of the military and naval forces of Virginia."

The rebel general, Gideon J. Pillow, sent a message to Parson Brownlow, inviting him to act as chaplain to his brigade, to which he received the following " spicy " reply : —

"KNOXVILLE, April 22, 1861.

" GEN. GIDEON J. PILLOW : — I have just received your message, through Mr. Sale, requesting me to serve as chaplain to your brigade in the Southern army ; and in the spirit of kindness in which this request is made, but in all candor, I return for an answer, that when I shall have made up my mind to go to hell, I will cut my throat and go direct, and not travel round by the way of the Southern Confederacy.

" I am very respectfully, &c.,.

" W. G. BROWNLOW."

A correspondent writing from Knoxville, under date of April 24, says : —

" The house of the celebrated, bold-hearted, and outspoken Parson Brownlow is the only one in Knoxville over which the stars and stripes are floating. A few days ago two armed secessionists went at six o'clock in the morning to haul down the stars and stripes. Miss Brownlow, a brilliant young lady of twenty-three, saw them on the piazza, and stepped out and demanded their business. They replied they had come to ' take down them stars and stripes.' She instantly drew a revolver from her side, and presenting it, said, ' Go on ! I'm good for one of you, and I think for both ! '

" ' By the look of that girl's eye she'll shoot,' one re-

16

marked. ' I think we'd better not try it; we'll go back and get more men,' said the other.

" ' Go and get more men,' said the noble lady; ' get more men and come and take it down, if you dare ! '

" They returned with a company of ninety armed men, and demanded that the flag should be hauled down. But on discovering that the house was filled with gallant men, armed to the teeth, who would rather die as dearly as possible than see their country's flag dishonored, the secessionists retired."

The common council of New York passed an order appropriating $1,000,000 to equip volunteers and provide for their families.

April 23.   General Butler took military possession of the Annapolis and Elk River Railroad.

At a flag-raising at Newburyport, a large American eagle was seen hovering over the assemblage.   The omen was hailed with cheers.   After which the large concourse assembled joined in singing " America."

The first regiment of South Carolina volunteers left Charleston for the seat of war on the Potomac.

April 24.   Governor Magoffin, of Kentucky, issued a proclamation calling on the State to place herself in a condition of defence.

April 25.   Fort Smith, in Arkansas, seized by rebels, under Solon Borland.

Major Sibley surrendered four hundred and fifty United States troops to the rebel Col. Van Dorn, at Saluria, Texas.

The Maryland legislature met at Frederick.   General Butler stated that if they passed an ordinance of secession he would arrest the entire body.   Governor Letcher, of Virginia, issued a proclamation announcing the transfer of the State to the government of the Southern Confederacy.

Senator Douglas made a speech before the .Illinois

legislature, urging immediate action in support of the government.

April 26. Governor Brown, of Georgia, issued a proclamation prohibiting the payment of Northern debts till the end of hostilities, and directing the payment of the money into the State treasury, to help defray the expenses of the war.

More bridges were burned near Baltimore, on the Philadelphia road.

April 27. General Scott was authorized by the President to suspend the writ of habeas corpus in the military district between Washington and Philadelphia, if found necessary to the public safety. Many Southerners employed in the departments at Washington resigned and left for the South, refusing to take the oath of allegiance. A steamer loaded with powder for the rebels was seized at Cairo.

The President issued a proclamation extending the blockade to the ports of Virginia and North Carolina.

While too much cannot be said in praise of the volunteers, from all parts of the country, their patriotic spirit and energy, yet Massachusetts troops seem to have a decided advantage in some respects over all others. They have so many apt and experienced mechanics among them, that they find no difficulty in laying down rails, building bridges, or running trains.

It was a fortunate dispensation that took Gen. Butler to Annapolis. His shrewd mind at once comprehended the importance of the position, and he set to work to make it secure. Not until that work was accomplished, did he allow troops to go forward. The malice of the secessionists was in one instance successfully baffled. The railroad men,-besides taking up the rails, had done considerable damage to the rolling stock. Gen. Butler sent a party, apparently unarmed, to the car-shop, who were met by the workmen, who refused them admittance.

Each Massachusetts man drew a "persuasive argument" from his breast, which operated like magic, and no further resistance was offered.

But another obstacle presented itself. The only engine in the building had been taken to pieces so thoroughly, that the author of the mischief asserted that no man north of the Potomac could put it together in two months. Our boys looked at the scene before them a minute; then one exclaimed, "I helped build that machine." Another said, "I'll bear a hand to put it together;" and a dozen others, who felt perfectly at home on the occasion, sprang forward, so that in a few hours the engine was under steam.

April 29. Maryland House of Delegates voted against secession, 53 to 13. The State senate published an address, signed by all the members, denying the intention of passing an ordinance of secession. Steamships Tennessee, Texas, and Hermes seized at New Orleans.

'April 30. A soldier who escaped from Charleston, states that the Southern stories of a bloodless fight in Charleston harbor are not true, — that he served at the guns during the fight at Fort Moultrie, and that nearly every shot from Fort Sumter killed somebody. Between three and four hundred were killed, and a large number wounded, at Fort Moultrie, during the siege.

The killed were collected in a mass and interred at night in Potter's field. Many were also killed in dwellings outside the fort. The soldiers were threatened with death if they disclosed the facts about the killed. People were constantly inquiring for their friends, and were assured they were at Sullivan's Island.

Another soldier who was at Morris Island says that one hundred and fifty were killed there, and forty at Sullivan's Island. He makes the same statement relative to the dead being buried at night in Potter's field.

We cannot of course *vouch* for the truth of this statement, though it would seem a "decided" miracle, if a bombardment of forty-eight hours could go on without killing somebody; especially, in a crowded fort, it would hardly be possible to throw shot or shell without hitting some one; whereas in Fort Sumter the garrison were so "few and far between," that, with precaution, they might escape.

All masters of vessels received notice on the twenty-fourth to leave Charleston in forty-eight hours, or they would be held by the Southern government. Some were detained for lack of men to work their ships, and the rest fled.

April 30.   Jefferson Davis sent a message to Congress at Montgomery, in which he stated that there were in the field, at Charleston and the forts in the South, 19,000 men, and 16,000 en route for Virginia.

Troops were constantly passing through Wilmington, from South Carolina and Georgia for Richmond.

Governor Ellis, of North Carolina, called for thirty thousand volunteers additional to the regular militia, and all organized corps were commanded to be in readiness at an hour's notice.

A Savannah paper of the 23d says: "There are three vessels here, ready fitted, waiting for privateer commissions, which will be received in a few days. They will be commanded by skilful seamen, and many others will sail under the charge of rebel Yankees.

"Recruits are fast pouring into Savannah, and great preparations are making to join the rebel army in the border States for an attack upon Washington. There is great excitement in Savannah, and all Unionism is effectually overawed."

The proclamation of President Davis to legalize piracy, the taunt and defiance bandied between sections, seemed as though madness ruled the hour, and that nothing but a conflict of arms — dreadful as the remedy is — could

16*

restore reason to its throne. In the noon of the nineteenth century, in this trial hour of our country's dire
calamity, we distrust *our* power to write aright, but as
the cloud thickens and lowers around us, we stand in the
faith that the God who smiled on the "heritage of the
fathers" will be with the sons, and direct them in their
efforts to save the country now. This is the "Light behind the cloud;" in this faith let the union of the loyal
men be perfect.

Europe has told us we were not a military people;
that partisan policy would triumph over government; but
the test has come, and party is forgotten. Political enemies in peace have become firm friends in war.

It is true, that, when the sixth decade of the nineteenth century came to an end, and the year 1861 was
ushered in, it found the North pursuing their usual quiet
avocations in peace and harmony; the entire free States,
from East to West, wholly unprepared for war, and no
extraordinary anxiety manifested in regard to an invasion
or a dissolution of the Union, and, notwithstanding the
foreshadowing of the coming storm, the North slumbered
on, until the lightnings from Sumter awoke them to the
stern reality that war had overtaken them and found
them sleeping;—no army; the military condition of the
country at the lowest ebb; no navy; no equipments;
no soldiers, with the exception of here and there an independent company, or an isolated regiment which had
become inactive from want of use. These were only a
"drop in the bucket;" but, simultaneously with the fall
of Sumter, an immense army sprang into existence, as
the growth of a single night. New England "blazed"
with musketry; New York arose in her might; Pennsylvania was awake, and the great North-west poured in her
sons to defend the country, and in the brief period of
a few weeks we have an army of two hundred thousand
men, preparing for the conflict to put down rebellion,

and subdue the enemies of the government. The plead-
ings are made up. The trial has commenced. Armed
hundreds of thousands are the jury; and the world is
the court.

We might describe at great length the noble conduct
of many; the services rendered; the generous donations
of moneyed men; the liberal and praiseworthy assistance
of the ladies in making garments for the soldiers and
providing them with little necessaries and comforts; the
tender of benefits, at places of amusement, for soldiers
and their families; the offers of express companies, railroad corporations and shipping merchants, to carry pack-
ages, letters and troops free of expense; of physicians,
to give medicine and attendance, free of charge, to the
families of those who had been called away; of heavy
loans to the government, from private citizens as well as
banking houses; of reduction of rents; of generous donations of ready-made clothing for soldiers; of handsome
contributions in churches; of the magnificent display of
flags and decorations by public and private individuals;
but we are inadequate to the task — we cannot do justice
to the subject. It would be impossible to particularize
without omitting the mention of many worthy individuals
whose patriotism was unsurpassed; suffice it to say, that
but one heart, one voice, one feeling predominated.
What was not done by government, was made up by
private individuals; the rich, as with one consent, lifted
upon their shoulders the burden of many families of
those who were gone or going, — assumed responsibilities, and poured out their money for the general good;
and to speak of decorations in national colors, we cannot
better express it than to say, men, women and children,
towns, cities and villages throughout the free States, literally "blazed" with red, white and blue.

CHAPTER X. ·

The cause is sacred in which they fell,
And holy the tears which flow. . . .

MAY 1. Wednesday. — The bodies of the Massachusetts men, A. O. Whitney and Luther C. Ladd, who died at Baltimore, were returned to the State from which they had so recently departed. Also, Sumner H. Needham, of Company I, Lawrence, who died from a wound (fracture of the skull) received in the attack on the troops at Baltimore.

Information was received at noon that the bodies were on their way to Boston, and instant preparations were made for their proper reception. The Independent Cadets were ordered out to do escort duty, and the call was promptly answered. At four o'clock they left their armory, under command of Major Baldwin, and marched to the depot of the Western Railroad. ·

The news of the expected arrival was announced in the Journal and other papers, and spread quickly; and a large concourse of citizens collected around the depot, anxiously awaiting the arrival of the train. Governor Andrew, accompanied by two of his aids, and Adjutant-General Schouler, with other gentlemen belonging to different departments of the State government, came in hacks to take the bodies into the charge of the State.

The train entered the depot at seven minutes of five, and the bodies, three in number, laid in metallic coffins, and then enclosed in pine boxes, were taken from the cars. They came in the care of Merrill S. Wright, a private of the Richardson Light Infantry, of Lowell, who

188

was detailed by Col. Jones, of the Sixth Regiment, for that purpose. He left Washington on Monday, arriving at Baltimore the same evening, and received the bodies from City Marshal Kane, in whose charge they were. No objection was made by any of the authorities of the city, and he left there Tuesday morning and came directly to Boston. Mr. Wright did not see the bodies, as the coffins had not been opened since they were put in, and could say nothing concerning the truth of the statement that they had been mutilated.

The bodies were placed upon biers which had been prepared, and each being covered by an American flag, they were borne into the street, where the Cadets had formed in line, and presented arms, while the band played " Pleyel's Hymn," and all the spectators stood reverentially with uncovered heads. The clouds, which had before darkened the heavens, broke suddenly away, and the sun looked down brightly upon the scene where thousands of citizens had gathered with sorrowful hearts to receive the bodies of the martyrs from Massachusetts who fell in the cause of government and law. Hearses were in attendance, in which the coffins were placed, and, surrounded by the Cadets, they moved slowly from the depot. The Governor and the gentlemen who accompanied him, with Mr. Wright, who had the bodies in charge, followed in carriages. The military marched with arms reversed, and the band played solemn dirges as the funeral cortege passed along the streets, which were crowded with people, all preserving a religious silence. The procession passed through Washington Street to West, and thence up Tremont to the State House, over the same spot as that on which they stood but two weeks before and received the banner in defence of which they had fought so bravely. No halt was made until, marching down Beacon Street, they reached King's Chapel, at the corner of School and Tremont Streets, in the vault of which the remains were

16*

deposited, with the same ceremonies which had characterized their reception at the depot.

COMMONWEALTH OF MASSACHUSETTS.

EXECUTIVE DEPARTMENT, COUNCIL CHAMBER, }
BOSTON, May 1, 1861. }

Hon. B. C. Sergeant, Mayor of Lowell: —

SIR : Mr. Merrill S. Wright, of Lowell, arrived at Boston this afternoon at five o'clock, in charge of the remains of those Massachusetts men who fell at Baltimore on the 19th of April. I met these relics of our brave and patriotic soldiers at the Worcester Railroad depot, accompanied by my military staff and the Executive Council, where we took them in charge, and, under the escort of the corps of Independent Cadets, bore them through our streets, thronged by sympathizing citizens, and placed them in the "Vassall" tomb beneath the ancient King's Chapel, at the corner of Tremont and School Streets. There they remain, subject to the orders of those friends who have the right to decide their final disposition. But it would be most grateful to the Executive Department, in coöperation with those nearest to the lamented dead, to assist in the last funeral honors to their memory ; and I should be pleased to meet you and the Mayor of Lawrence and the Selectmen of Stoneham, as soon as you may convene them, at the State House, to consider the arrangements suitable to the occasion.

I am, yours respectfully,

JOHN A. ANDREW, *Governor.*

During the passage of the procession through the streets the flags on the City Hall and at other points were displayed at half-mast; and several stores on Washington Street—Macullar, Williams & Parker, Kinmonth & Co., George Turnbull & Co., H. M. Smith, Raymond & Cary, G. W. Warren & Co., Washington Building, Shreve, Brown & Co., Williams & Everett, and others—

were draped in black, and showed other emblems of mourning.

The American flag was raised on the steeple of the Old South Church, Boston, with appropriate ceremonies.

The steam transport Cambridge sailed with supplies for the Massachusetts troops at Fort Monroe, Annapolis and Washington, and about one hundred and fifty troops for the seat of war, including Captain Dodd's company of Rifles, nineteen recruits for the New Bedford City Guards at Fort Monroe, ten men for the Taunton Light Guard, and forty-two recruits for Company K, Third Regiment, stationed at Fort Monroe. She carried, in addition to the volunteer troops, a squad of twelve picked men, from the United States Marine corps, to act as a permanent guard to the steamer. The troops were supplied with forty thousand rounds of musket and rifle cartridges, and ammunition for the rifled cannon and broadside guns. The troops, glowing with health and youthful enthusiasm, were in the best possible spirits, and, as the steamer glided into the stream, returned with hearty cheers the parting salutations of their friends. When fairly clear of the wharf, a salute was fired from a heavy broadside gun.

Governor Buckingham, of Connecticut, in his message, recommends an efficient State militia; says that forty-one volunteer companies have already been accepted, and the Fifth Regiment will soon be full; that all parties are acting in harmony on the question; and, referring to the attitude of the South, he remarks:—

" The alternative of submitting to their claims, or to the overthrow of the government, is now presented. The issue is forced upon us, and must be met; not by cowardice and humble subserviency to usurped authority, but by firmness corresponding with the magnitude of the interests at hazard, and in a spirit that shall vindicate the insulted majesty of a nation. The sceptre of authority must be upheld, and allegiance secured. It is no time to make concession to rebels, or parley with men in arms. We must make no sacrifices of principles vital to freedom, and no indecent haste for conciliation and peace. 'God makes haste slowly.'

"This is the day of our trial. Freedom and despotism, republicanism and absolutism, civilization and religion, from every corner of this earth, are watching with intense interest, as we vibrate between law and anarchy. . .

"But indifferent or disloyal we cannot be. Fail or falter we shall not. Through and beyond the clouds and darkness of the present I think I see a bright and glorious future. I hear, too, above the roar and shock of battle, prophetic voices — voices of the patriot dead, who fell at Lexington and Concord and Bunker Hill, and on every bloody field of the Revolution. They bid us look over this broad land, with its teeming millions, and all its wealth of prosperity, and to remember that it is the purchase of their blood. What they did for themselves, their children, and us, their children's children, they call on us to do for ourselves and ours. The liberties they conquered have been to us a proud heritage of freedom and national renown for more than three-quarters of a century. Be it ours to reconquer those liberties, and, by the blessing of God, transmit them, unimpaired, as a priceless legacy to those who come after us."

END OF VOL. I.

CPSIA information can be obtained
at www.ICGtesting.com
Printed in the USA
BVHW040947280319

543963BV00021B/454/P